SAINT NIKIFOROS
THE LEPER & WONDERWORKER

SAINT NIKIFOROS
THE LEPER & WONDERWORKER

BY SIMON THE MONK

*Translated and edited by the Sisters of
the Monastery of the Theotokos
The Life Giving Spring*

GREEK ORTHODOX MONASTERY OF THE THEOTOKOS
THE LIFE GIVING SPRING

2016

Ο ΑΓΙΟΣ ΝΙΚΗΦΟΡΟΣ Ο ΛΕΠΡΟΣ – Ο ΘΑΥΜΑΤΟΥΡΓΟΣ
Copyright © *Σίμων Μοναχός (Simon the Monk)*
Κυρίλλου Λουκάρεως 6, 114 71 ΑΘΗΝΑ
Τηλ: 210-6449.300, Fax: 210-6424.266
www.athoniki-politeia.gr
www.agiosnikiforos.gr
ΙΕΡΑ ΚΑΛΥΒΗ ΚΟΙΜΗΣΕΩΣ ΤΗΣ ΘΕΟΤΟΚΟΥ
ΣΚΗΤΗ ΚΟΥΤΛΟΥΜΟΥΣΙΟΥ, 630 86 ΚΑΡΥΑΙ, ΑΓΙΟΝ ΟΡΟΣ

First English edition Copyright 2016
© Greek Orthodox Monastery of the Theotokos
The Life Giving Spring
P.O. Box 549
Dunlap, California 93621 USA
PH: (559) 338-3110   FAX: (559) 338-3101

English book rights for publication and distribution in the USA and Canada are exclusively assigned to the Greek Orthodox Monastery of the Theotokos the Life Giving Spring.

ISBN 978-0-9851915-7-3

PRINTED IN THE UNITED STATES OF AMERICA

CONTENTS

HIS MEMORY IS
CELEBRATED ON THE

4TH

OF JANUARY

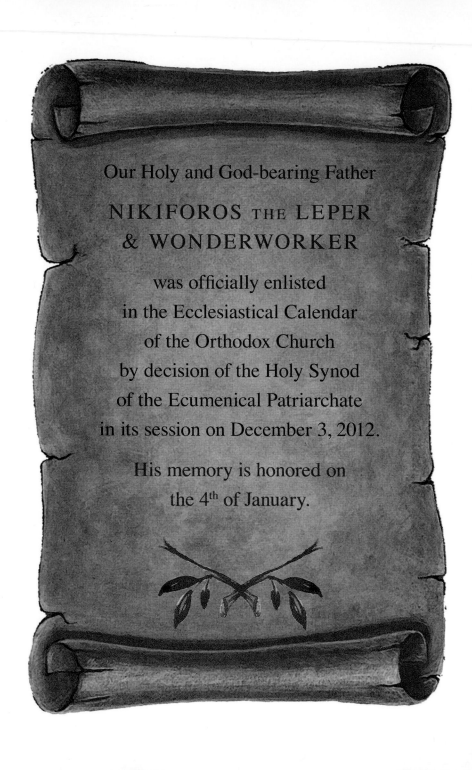

Our Holy and God-bearing Father

NIKIFOROS the LEPER & WONDERWORKER

was officially enlisted
in the Ecclesiastical Calendar
of the Orthodox Church
by decision of the Holy Synod
of the Ecumenical Patriarchate
in its session on December 3, 2012.

His memory is honored on
the 4th of January.

ΕΛΛΗΝΙΚΗ ΔΗΜΟΚΡΑΤΙΑ

Η ΙΕΡΑ ΣΥΝΟΔΟΣ
ΤΗΣ ΕΚΚΛΗΣΙΑΣ ΤΗΣ ΕΛΛΑΔΟΣ

Δ/νσις: Ἰωάννου Γενναδίου 14 - 115 21, Ἀθῆναι
Τηλ. 210-7272.204, Fax 210-7272.210, e-mail: contact@ecclesia.gr

ΠΡΩΤ. 195
ΑΡΙΘΜ.
ΔΙΕΚΠ. 295

ΑΘΗΝΗΣΙ 12η Φεβρουαρίου 2013

ΕΓΚΥΚΛΙΟΝ ΣΗΜΕΙΩΜΑ

Πρός
Τήν Ἱεράν Ἀρχιεπισκοπήν Ἀθηνῶν καί
Τάς Ἱεράς Μητροπόλεις τῆς Ἐκκλησίας τῆς Ἑλλάδος

ΘΕΜΑ : «Ἐνημέρωσις περί τῆς Ἀποφάσεως τοῦ Οἰκουμενικοῦ Πατριαρχείου διά τήν ἀναγραφήν ἐν ταῖς Ἁγιολογικαῖς Δέλτοις τῆς Ἁγίας ἡμῶν Ἐκκλησίας τοῦ μοναχοῦ Νικηφόρου τοῦ Λεπροῦ».

Ἐκ Συνοδικῆς Ἀποφάσεως, ληφθείσης ἐν τῇ Συνεδρίᾳ τῆς Διαρκοῦς Ἱερᾶς Συνόδου τῆς 8ης μηνός Φεβρουαρίου ἐ.ἔ., εὐαρέστως γνωρίζομεν ὑμῖν, ὅτι ὑπό τῆς ἐν Κωνσταντινουπόλει Ἁγίας τοῦ Χριστοῦ Μεγάλης Ἐκκλησίας, συνωδά τῇ κρατούσῃ πράξει καί τάξει τῆς Ἁγίας ἡμῶν Ἐκκλησίας, ἀνεγράφη προσφάτως ἐν ταῖς Ἁγιολογικαῖς Δέλτοις τῆς Ἐκκλησίας ὁ Μοναχός Νικηφόρος ὁ Λεπρός, τῆς μνήμης αὐτοῦ ἑορταζομένης τῇ δ΄ Ἰανουαρίου ἑκάστου ἔτους, ἐκδοθείσης ἐπί τούτῳ Πατριαρχικῆς καί Συνοδικῆς Πράξεως.

Τήν Κανονικήν ταύτην Ἀπόφασιν τῆς ἐν Κωνσταντινουπόλει Ἐκκλησίας ἀνακοινούμενοι ὑμῖν, παρακαλοῦμεν διά τά καθ' ὑμᾶς.

Ἐντολῇ τῆς Ἱερᾶς Συνόδου
Ὁ Ἀρχιγραμματεύς

† Ὁ Διαυλείας Γαβριήλ

The encyclical from the Church of Greece officially announcing the canonization of Saint Nikiforos the Leper.

Apolytikion. 1ˢᵗ Tone. *The stone that had been sealed.*

All the angels were awestruck by the courage and fortitude
of Saint Nikiforos the Leper in ascetic deeds and contests,
for like another Job he suffered pains
with patience, ever glorifying God,
who has crowned him now with glory, granting him grace
to work great, wondrous miracles.
Rejoice, O guide of monastics and their aid,
Rejoice, O shining beacon of light,
Rejoice, for your relics now exude a fragrance bringing
    joy to all.

Kontakion. Plagal 4ᵗʰ Tone. *O Champion General.*

The valiant athlete of endurance and of fortitude,
the steadfast diamond of great patience and longsuffering
who was tried by the affliction and pains of illness,
and who in this way did glorify the Most High God,
let us praise and laud the leper Nikiforos,
saying unto him:
Rejoice, true namesake of victory.

Megalynarion

O pious assembly, lovers of Christ,
now with hymns and praises, as is fitting, let us extol
the true friend of Christ God, the leper Nikiforos,
as a most wondrous athlete of holy fortitude.

PREFACE
TO THE
ENGLISH EDITION

n July of 2008, our close acquaintance, the pious priest Father Evangelos Xenitakis from Crete, visited our Monastery of the Life Giving Spring in California. He brought a small laminated icon of Saint Nikiforos the Leper that had a few tiny fragments of his holy relics sealed in the corner.

This is how I met the saint for the first time. His icon made a deep impression on me and I placed it inside the Holy Altar where we keep holy relics. Every Saturday when we would bring out the holy relics for the faithful to venerate, my desire grew for our monastery to obtain a more substantial portion of Saint Nikiforos' relics. At last, in the year 2013 I contacted Father Evangelos and he told me to communicate with Father Simon, the monk who had them in his possession. When I called Father Simon, he asked that we send an official letter stating the monastery's request for the saint's holy relics. I wrote it without delay, and he kindly responded.

In Father Simon's attempt to cut a piece of Saint Nikiforos' relics, he realized that they could only be cut in the way the saint himself wanted his relics to be given to us. They were placed in a special reliquary box and we received them at our monastery with all due honor. It is especially noteworthy that the saint arrived just before the building permit for the extension of our monastery—after many delays—was finally issued. His presence granted us new strength and encouragement. Since then, we bring out his holy relics every Saturday for the faithful to venerate. However, our communication and relationship with Saint Nikiforos did not stop at this.

When we began construction, I took the saint's icon and tied it to a branch of a tree next to the site. At the same time, I prayed and made a "contract" with him saying, "My saint, I have no idea how this building is going to be completed, neither from a technical nor from a financial standpoint. So listen, I'm putting you in charge—you are going to be the foreman. During your life you were not able to walk but now I want you to walk around and oversee the construction, making sure that everything proceeds correctly." From that time, my brethren, the icon of the saint remains on the branch and the construction proceeds—slowly but surely—with his supervision and through his intercessions. Now that we have painted our own icon of him, I take it outside every Monday and make the sign of the Cross with it over the construction site and over the workers for their safety. Great is the grace of the saint!

According to monastic tradition, a reading takes place during the common meal for spiritual benefit. Inspired by the presence of the saint we had chosen to read his biography, written by Father Simon, which we had received along with the relics. I was deeply moved by the saint's life, and thought, "Wouldn't it be wonderful if this book were translated into English, the language spoken by the people here?" Once again I took courage and called Father Simon—not for relics this time, but for his blessing to translate the book. When he told me that he had already made other arrangements, I accepted it as the will of God. However, I did not completely give up hope.

Many months had passed when I received an un-expected phone call from Father Simon inquiring if we were still interested in translating the book. I immediately responded that it would be our great joy. This is how we began and with the grace of God, and of the saint, we have now finished. We thank Saint Nikiforos for strengthening and inspiring the sisters throughout the work of translation. I believe it will touch the souls of English speakers just as it spoke to our own hearts—that they, too, might come to know the saint and develop a relationship with him, calling upon him in every necessity, for health, assistance and salvation.

I would like to express my deepest gratitude to Father Simon who gave us this honor, blessing and opportunity. May God and Saint Nikiforos grant him long life and salvation. In closing, we pray that the saint might always continue to intercede on behalf of the sisterhood of the Holy Monastery of the Life Giving Spring.

With many prayers and blessings,
the lowly Abbess Markella together with the sisters,
Monastery of the Theotokos the Life Giving Spring
Dunlap, California

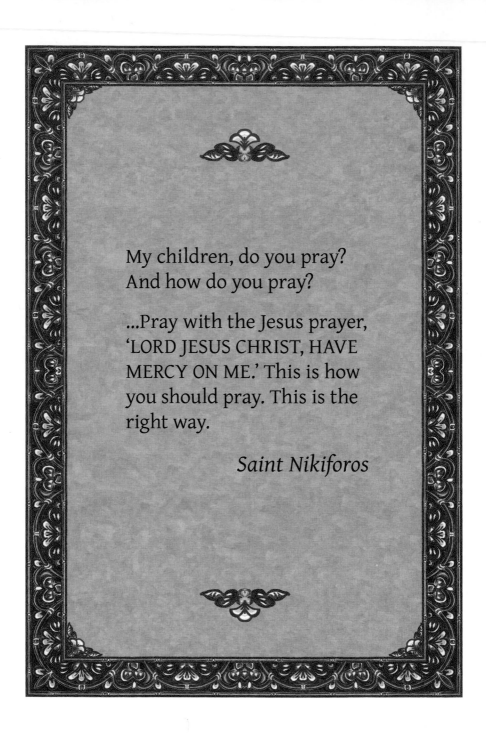

My children, do you pray?
And how do you pray?

...Pray with the Jesus prayer,
'LORD JESUS CHRIST, HAVE
MERCY ON ME.' This is how
you should pray. This is the
right way.

Saint Nikiforos

INTRODUCTION

any years ago, I began visiting the Leprosy Treatment Center of Athens, spending as much time as I could with the pained and suffering people who lived there. I came to know them well and a close bond developed between us. They were people marked by the torments of illness and abandonment, but also by the blessed virtue of humility. Through their faith and hope in God, and through their great patience (many of them were maimed and disabled), they had been purified and filled with God's grace.

It was there that I came to know the most holy elder Evmenios, who later became my much respected and very beloved spiritual father, a man "full of grace and the Holy Spirit" (cf. Acts 6:5), with great virtues and spiritual gifts.

My Pappouli[1] had as his spiritual guide a great yet hidden saint, Father Nikiforos. He too was a leper, but

---

[1] "Pappouli" in Greek is an endearing name for a priest or monk.

full of divine fragrance; blind, but beholding the noetic light and heavenly revelations; paralyzed, but unceasingly watchful and praying. That is why his holy relics are fragrant.

I felt it was my sacred duty to present and make known to the whole body of the Church this glorious vessel of grace, this bright star of all virtues and especially of patience, this earthly angel and heavenly man. Relying on the prayers of the saint and having received a blessing from my spiritual father, I began this endeavor. The undertaking was quite a difficult one. And yet, from the very outset, I witnessed the assistance of the holy Father.

Father Nikiforos was born in 1890 and reposed in 1964. Immediate relatives, siblings and cousins, who would have been able to provide invaluable information about him, were no longer alive. Likewise, most of those who knew him at the Leper Communities of Chios and of Athens had also passed on. Those remaining were scattered throughout all of Greece, the Holy Mountain, and abroad. I searched and found a few people who had known him personally. One person led me to the next like the links of a chain, as if the saint's own holy hand was directing me. Although my mission was small, it was quite difficult—involving great distances and requiring much time and toil. But may glory be given to God, for with the help of our Panagia[2] and of our holy Father, all went well.

---

[2] "Panagia" is a Greek word meaning "all-holy one" and is used to refer to the Virgin Mary.

I owe much gratitude to my reverend spiritual father for the support and encouragement he provided during the writing and completion of the present work. I also warmly thank His Eminence Metropolitan Efthymios of Acheloos, His Eminence Metropolitan Nikiforos of Lefkas and Ithaca, His Eminence Metropolitan Neophytos of Morphou, the Very Reverend Archimandrite Nikodemos Giannakopoulos, the reverend monk Justus, and the most respected John Spyropoulos, all of whom sent their written testimonies with great eagerness.

I express the same thanks likewise to all the venerable and beloved fathers and brethren who toiled and helped with the collection and cross-checking of the elements of this work, and who in various ways contributed to its publication.

May the Lord God remember the love and eagerness with which all of these people offered their contributions.

I close with the humble and heartfelt wish that our God-bearing Father might always intercede to the Lord on behalf of all who reverently read his sacred life.

Written in the Holy Skete of
Saint Panteleimon, Mount Athos,
following the feast of our Panagia,[3]
in the month of August, the year of our Lord 2003,
by the least among monks, Simon

---

[3] The feast of Panagia's Dormition is celebrated on the 15th of August.

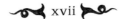 xvii

Abba Agathon said:

"If it were possible for me to find a leper and to give him my body and take his own for myself, I would do so gladly, for this is perfect love."

from the Gerontikon

THE RIGHTEOUS
LIVE FOREVER[1]

I f pain, afflictions, and trials were eliminated from the life of man, holiness would belong only to the angels. This truth, which is an axiom of our Orthodox faith, was known well by Father Nikiforos Tzanakakis who departed to the Lord on January 4, 1964. Nicholas, as he was called before his monastic tonsure, was born in Crete in 1887[2] to pious parents. Stricken with leprosy, he came to see it not as a curse, but as a special favor from heaven and a personal calling from Christ, the One who sets the contest. So it was that at the age of 17 he had departed from his homeland and gone to venerate the Holy Places—especially

---

[1] A moving eulogy, true and full of grace, delivered at the solemn repose of the holy Father by a likewise holy man, his affectionate spiritual son Monk Sophronios – later the spiritual father, Hieromonk Evmenios.

[2] Although in the narrative we refer to the year of his birth as 1890, we preserve here the year as recorded in the publication of the eulogy.

the Place of the Skull,[3] where pain was wholly sanctified, making Golgotha a symbol for those who emerge victorious in the midst of life's afflictions and adversities. It was from there, from that inexhaustible ocean of courage and fortitude, that he drew the courage and patience that enabled him to hold high—very high—his own cross for all of 52 years.

In 1912, he was admitted to the Leper Community of Chios and tonsured a monk by the holy Father Anthimos Vayianos. Who can enumerate his beautiful spiritual struggles in this new life? Although his body was deteriorating day by day, the inner man was being rejuvenated. The illness was destroying the members of his body—eyes, hands and feet—so that in the end he remained immobile. Yet this praiseworthy man was destroying every conceivable passion and vice, reaching blessed dispassion and perfect obedience to the will of God and to his spiritual father, becoming a man of most fervent prayer par excellence.

Neither did he lack in any way the gift of preaching. Though he did not speak with strong words, his aforesaid virtues and his noble, broad smile preached more effectively than the strongest preacher. For this reason his cell had become a font of spiritual rebirth; it was there that both healthy and ailing people found courage. Orthodox

---

[3] The pilgrimage site of Golgotha in Jerusalem, which translates "the Place of the Skull," is where Jesus Christ was crucified, on top of the historic location of the skull of the first man, Adam.

 xx

clergy who were very highly educated considered even one visit with Father Nikiforos to be a blessing from God. For all of them, and for us, Father Nikiforos was a spiritual oasis in the Sahara desert of our life. And so his repose casts us into unspeakable sadness, but it also brings us joy because we believe that we now have a fervent intercessor before the Lord to protect us from the traps of the evil one.

May your holy memory be eternal, for the righteous live forever.

Your most lowly spiritual child,
Sophronios, Monk of Saint Niketas' Monastery

A LIFE
WELL-PLEASING
TO GOD

n 1890, Nicholas Tzanakakis was born on the island
of Crete, in the village of Sirikari. He came to be
called Father Nikiforos, as a monk of the Orthodox
Church, and his island of Crete, which has given
birth to many saints, boasts of bringing forth yet another
elect child of God.

The village of Sirikari, in the western region of
Chania, is known for the Tsichlian Gorge with its amazing
natural beauty and the special celebration of the feast of
Panagia's Dormition that takes place on the 15th of August.
This mountainous village has a healthy climate. Beautiful
forests contain an abundance of chestnut trees, surround
rich bodies of water, and envelop gorges and caves. The
village itself has a unique characteristic to its design: it
is divided into eleven neighborhoods, each bearing the
name of the first family to dwell there. Each family also

built a church in their neighborhood in honor of their patron saint. For this reason, the village, to this day, has thirteen churches. The newborn Nicholas Tzanakakis first saw the light of day in the neighborhood of the Kostogiannides family, where there are three churches: one dedicated to the Dormition of the Theotokos, another to the Archangels Michael and Gabriel, and a third to Saint Ephraim.

It was in this village that the infant Nicholas' first cries were heard. It was here that he shed the first innocent tears of his childhood. Later his tears were to become tears of pain, and still later they would become tears of spiritual joy. The latter sprung from unceasing prayer and from his union with his most beloved Lord, the Lord of patience and consolation.

The First Years

His parents, John and Glykeria, were very pious and simple people. They were known for their faithfulness, a common characteristic among the Sirikarian villagers, and raised their children in the teachings and shelter of the church. Nicholas' mother was fondly called a "Hatzina" as an honorary title given to someone who has made a pilgrimage to the Holy Land and been baptized in the Jordan River. Every summer, Nicholas' family would gather with the whole village in his own neighborhood at the church dedicated to the Dormition of the Mother of God for the renowned celebration on the 15th of August. The

The village of Sirikari today

The childhood home of Saint Nikiforos in Sirikari

village community was blessed to have many churches in which they could offer true prayer and worship to God. Nicholas, however, was not to enjoy this blessed warmth of a spiritual upbringing and loving family for very long. At a very young age he and his siblings were orphaned. The little children were deprived of their mother's warm embrace and their father's guiding hand. The villagers, relatives and godparents stepped forth in Christian love to care for the orphans, but the pain of losing their parents brought many difficulties and scarred their tender, early years.

Little Nicholas was taken to live with his grandfather, John Tzanakakis, who raised his dear grandson to the best of his ability. Under his guidance, Nicholas was able to receive an elementary education at the primary school in the village.

When Nicholas was only thirteen years old, he left his home and this familiar, warm family environment, his beloved siblings and the young friends and playmates he grew up with. Unbeknownst to him at the time, he would never return to them. He would never see again his brothers and sisters. He would never behold again the beauty of the Sirikari mountains, the churches of his village, nor the graves of his parents.

His grandfather, looking out with love and concern for the young boy's future, brought Nicholas to Chania to work at a barbershop. John saw fit to bring him from their little village to the nearby city where Nicholas could learn a trade and secure a livelihood. Naturally, the living conditions there in the big city were not ideal for a young village boy who was alone and without protection. Nicholas, however, had a magnetic personality. He was clever, tall and handsome. Despite the painful loss of his beloved parents in his early years, he was very sociable. Everybody loved him and he, likewise, always took joy in the people around him.

However, in the arena of life, a most difficult and painful contest awaited him, greater than he could ever have imagined. At some point, alone in the city, not long after he had begun working, he noticed a small blemish on his skin, encircled by a thin ring. It was the first indication that he had contracted leprosy. Sometimes called the "holy" illness, likely because of its mention in the Holy Bible, the initial sign was characterized by this persistent blemish and thin ring. For Nicholas, this was a sign that he had been given a heavy cross. And not only was he to bear this heavy cross, but it was also to be the seal of his martyrdom. As time passed, he would come to understand this all the more.

> LEPROSY today is usually referred to as "Hansen's disease," after the Norwegian physician Gerhard Armauer Hansen, who discovered in 1873 the bacterium that causes the illness. Leprosy is mentioned often in Holy Scripture (cf. Leviticus 13:1-14:57, Matthew 8:1-14, Mark 1:40-44, Luke 5:12-14, 17:12-19). It was always considered a dreadful,

contagious disease. For this reason, lepers were re-
garded with great fear and treated with hostility and
aversion. Historically, outbreaks of leprosy were only
controlled by isolating and eliminating those who
were unfortunate enough to have caught it. Only in
recent years have lepers become accepted in society.
This is due, in part, to the advance of medical science
that discovered the cure for leprosy, but also to the
Frenchman Raoul Follereau and others who made
great efforts to enlighten the public concerning the
illness.

THE PATRON SAINT of lepers is Saint Zoticus, the
feeder of orphans, whose memory is honored on
December 31st. Saint Zoticus lived in Constantinople
and was a member of the imperial court. When
leprosy broke out in the city, a law was made dictating
that anyone found to be affected by the disease must
be drowned in the sea. Saint Zoticus was greatly
saddened by this and tried to devise a way to save
the lepers. He approached the Emperor Constantius
(son of Constantine the Great) and, appealing to his
vanity, asked for large sums of money, supposedly
for the purchase of precious stones to decorate the
palace. With this money, he would purchase from
the executioners the release of the condemned lepers
and establish them in a place that he had founded
specially for them. After some time, a famine broke out
in Constantinople. When the Emperor inquired as to
the cause, certain ill-willed men reported that Zoticus
was responsible, since he was taking the Emperor's

money and caring for the lepers. Upon hearing this accusation, the Emperor asked the saint to show him the precious stones that he was supposedly buying. The saint in turn brought the Emperor to see the lepers, whom he had instructed beforehand to await the monarch's arrival and greet him ceremoniously with lit candles in hand. The first among them was the Emperor's own daughter whom the saint had also ransomed, redeeming her from being drowned in the sea. As soon as the Emperor saw them, he became furious and commanded that the saint be tied behind wild mules, which were beaten so that they would run until the saint was torn to pieces. After the saint gave up his soul, the Emperor's men continued to strike the mules, until the mules spoke with human voices and rebuked the hard-heartedness and inhumanity of the monarch. After this miraculous occurrence, the Emperor Constantius repented. He had a large hospital built for the lepers in that place, together with a church in honor and memory of the saint.

DURING THE 9TH CENTURY AD, it was Saracen invaders who first brought the dreadful disease of leprosy to the island of Crete. Those affected by the disease were outcast and would live by begging. They slept in caves outside of the cities and villages, or in abandoned houses. In 1903, the high commissioner Prince George encountered some of them himself, as they were seeking alms outside of Chania. He then conceived the idea of allocating the island of Spinalonga to those who were suffering from leprosy—a plan he indeed put into effect.

PEOPLE WERE SUFFERING from this disease throughout the rest of the Greek islands as well, because the inhabitants would come into contact with the Saracens and others who carried leprosy. The island of Chios was the first to establish a Leper Community—an isolated hospital community for people with leprosy. It was founded in the year 1378 and later restored in 1909. However, it served exclusively the lepers who were natives of the island. As is narrated later, Saint Anthimos, the priest of the Leper Community of Chios, "foreseeing something better" (cf. Hebrews 11:40), paid a considerable sum of money for the institution to accept Father Nikiforos who was from another part of Greece.

IN THOSE YEARS, around the turn of the century, many people were suffering from Hansen's disease. Anyone could be affected, from young children to adults. Oftentimes, more than one member of the same family was afflicted. Regardless of age or social position, all were rejected by society and cast away. They had to distance themselves from their home, their neighborhood, their friends, and their relatives. Parents had to leave behind their own children so as not to infect them. Little children would be separated from their siblings and severed from their parents. Naturally this gave rise to many difficulties. This permanent separation caused unbearable pain, and the rejection and alienation left grievous consequences in the subsequent lives of the lepers and their families. But our Holy God, who gave them this heavy cross, also gave them the strength to carry it. They were crowned and glorified by Him not only for their patience in suffering, but also for being cast out to suffer alone. We who are healthy, however, will be judged by Him as to whether or not we showed any consideration or compassion for them. We will be judged for our horrific failure to show them heartfelt love and sympathy. We should shed many tears at the thought that we readily exiled these pained children of God. We sent away these brothers of Christ, our very own brothers, to distant and parched islands. As a society, we shut them within high walls and locked them behind heavy doors so that we would not be contaminated by their sickness.

Young Nicholas was deeply disturbed and extremely worried when he discovered the symptoms of leprosy on his skin. All of a sudden, this little child of thirteen grew up. His circumstances forced him to mature abruptly. His spontaneous laughter was cut short and his carefree childhood joys came to an end. From that moment on, any time he laughed or played it was all feigned and affected. He only pretended to display any sort of merriment characteristic of his young age so that those around him would not catch on to his big secret.

Like all his young companions, he was very familiar with the symptoms of the disease because of the frequent examinations by the school doctors and the regional medical officers. He was also well aware of the dreadful consequences if the authorities were to learn of his condition: persecution, isolation, and confinement on Spinalonga.

For a long time he took care to conceal the parts of his body where the symptoms of leprosy had appeared. He was living out his own personal drama every day, in total secrecy and completely alone. A shudder would pass through his whole body at the horrifying thought that he might be caught and confined on Spinalonga.

> SPINALONGA—at one time referred to as "the grave of the living dead"—is a small island in the Mirabello Gulf, across from the town of Saint Nicholas on Crete. The island took its name from the Venetians, who had corrupted a Greek phrase describing a nearby location on the mainland. On this island, as the high commissioner Prince George arranged, a leper colony was established in 1904. From that time, it was given over exclusively to those "condemned." For 53 years (1904-1957), the island was sanctified by the martyrdom of countless, nameless lepers. This forsaken place was made holy by their tears, their sighs, their pains, and their patience.

By the time Nicholas was 16 years old, the signs of his disease were becoming much more visible. Willing to make any effort necessary to avoid the dreaded confinement on Spinalonga, he left Crete. Discreetly, in secret and in silence, he boarded a boat bound for Egypt. In 1906, he arrived in Alexandria.

> ALEXANDRIA, the great ancient city of Egypt, was built in the 3rd century BC by the architects of Alexander the Great, Deinocrates and Naucratides. The famous temple of Artemis at Ephesus is also attributed to them. The city of Alexandria flourished both spiritually and economically, especially during the Hellenistic period. The Evangelist Mark (†AD 63) taught in this city, and became its first hierarch. Spiritual life in Alexandria contributed much to the spread and development of Christianity. In the 19th century and the beginning of the 20th, there was a thriving Greek community in the city.

In Alexandria, young Nicholas was able to find work at a barbershop. Practicing the trade he learned in his homeland, Crete, he was able to meet the expenses of his residence and subsistence. In this way he prudently avoided becoming a burden to anyone. Regardless of his difficult childhood, Nicholas remained very sociable and was loved by all. He became known within the flourishing Greek community, and was acquainted with the priests and hierarchs of the Patriarchal See of Alexandria. Many of the people he encountered helped him to adapt to his new environment. They supported him greatly, enabling him to become acclimated and accustomed to a new life in a foreign country among strangers—people with an unfamiliar language, with different customs and religion.

The Patriarchate of Alexandria

They also helped him fulfill the great desire of his soul—
to visit the Holy Land and venerate the Holy Places.

Nicholas' leprosy, however, continued to progress.
The miserable, debilitating disease was working its
damage throughout the young man's body. At that critical
point in time, the cure for leprosy had yet to be discovered.
It would take medical science another 40 years to offer
hope to those suffering and dying. Until 1947, when the
cure was finally found, a diagnosis of leprosy meant that
a painful, agonizing death was inevitable.

Over time, as was to be expected, Nicholas' sores
became more and more visible. Their gruesome appearance was becoming especially prevalent on his hands
and face. After seven or eight years in Alexandria, in his
early twenties, they had become significantly more pro-
nounced. This condition was extremely problematic for
the poor young man. He was becoming more and more
uneasy and apprehensive with each passing day. He did
not know what to do. He did not know how to hide.

Nicholas did not want his condition to be noticed by
the people or the local authorities. If he were apprehend-
ed, he was sure that they would send him back to Crete.
He was certain that he should somehow depart from
Alexandria and go to another place. But where could he
go, and how was he to get there? Though he had met so
many people, he had no one. While he had worked and
provided for himself, he still had no means to help himself in this dire situation. Affliction and worry were his

Saint Nikiforos as a young man in Alexandria

constant companions and daily sustenance. Plagued with a relentless fear, the same question repeated itself over and over in his mind: "At any moment now, someone who knows the symptoms of leprosy is going to expose me and betray me to the authorities and then how will I escape? What will I do?" The laws concerning leprosy at that time were very strict and made no exceptions. Nicholas had no answers, and could find no solution. He would go numb at the thought that he, a young man in the prime of his life, might pass the rest of his days locked up and isolated on the arid island of Spinalonga. There he would be nothing and do nothing but wait until the end.

Enlightened by the all-merciful God, Nicholas finally confided his anguish to a hierarch at the Patriarchate who was from Chios. The hierarch set Nicholas' tormented mind at rest. His grace-filled words gave him courage and support. He embraced him with abundant love and understanding. He acted as only a genuine, true father would act towards his own son. This blessed hierarch understood that he was dealing with a soul who, though certainly pained and distressed, was also pure and upright. He had before him an extraordinary person. Nicholas was not one of this world, but one upon whom the grace of the Holy Spirit rested.

For this reason, he decided immediately to make contact with his acquaintance, Father Anthimos Vayianos (now known as Saint Anthimos), the priest who served the Leper Community on the island of Chios. He wrote to him about young Nicholas. He explained the condition of his illness but also his exceptional manners and character. He described his impeccable conduct and behavior throughout all the years he lived in Alexandria. Father Anthimos received the recommendation and gave notice that Nicholas should be sent to him straightaway. Indeed, within a short period of time, his words were put into effect.

λ Leper in Chios

The hierarch not only provided Nicholas with a beautiful letter of recommendation, but also paid for his ticket to Chios. He would be travelling first to Smyrna from Alexandria and then to the island. Along with his fatherly blessings, the hierarch also gave him enough money to cover his initial expenses. With true love and compassion, he accompanied him to the port and bid farewell to his young friend.

With a heavy heart, Nicholas left the great city of Alexandria. He left behind all the beloved friends he had come to know there. And where was he going, but to the unknown. To unknown people, unknown places, and an unknown environment. Once again his life would change. Once again he had taken to flight. Once again he was uprooted and displaced. His heart wrenched with the pain of his departure. He held back his tears for fear that they would run endlessly. Nevertheless, he knew that this was how it had to be. It was essential for him to leave, and for it be done as quickly and discreetly as possible, before his dreadful secret became known. Once again he needed to gather both the courage and strength to carry on.

Setting straight his thoughts, and with unshakeable faith that his beloved Jesus would continue to be with him, he boarded the ship and departed. After a toilsome journey of some days' time, he arrived at Çeçme, a small city on the shores of Turkey across from Chios. The city's Greek name was Krine, and at that time it had 17,000 inhabitants of whom 15,000 were Greeks. Father Anthimos himself was waiting to greet the tired young man when he arrived. Having formally made his acquaintance, he took Nicholas aboard a small boat. Together they sailed the short distance that separated the mainland from the island of Chios. It was there that Nicholas would spend the next 43 years of his life. Within this time he would experience his best and most spiritual years, as the following narrative reveals. He arrived in Chios in 1914, at the age of 24.

THE ISLAND OF CHIOS was occupied by the Persians during the 6th century BC, and later freed by the Athenians. During the time of the Byzantine Empire, Chios served as the military headquarters of the Aegean. The Turks had conquered the island, but it was freed from them in the year 1912. As one of the larger Greek islands, it now has an established Orthodox Metropolis and many holy monasteries, both for men and women. The oldest is thought to be

The buildings of the Leper Community of Chios as they look today

Another view of the buildings that housed the Leper Community

"Nea Moni" or "New Monastery" (founded in 1042), and one of the newer monasteries is that which Father Anthimos founded in 1930, "Panagia the Helper." The island's soil has been watered with the blood of thousands of martyrs, including many new-martyrs and those who died for their country. Among the most well-known of these martyrs are Saint Markella and Saint Isidore. Martyred in the 3rd century, Saint Isidore is considered the patron saint of Chios and his memory is honored on May 14th. Noteworthy as well on the island are the mastic trees, unique in the world, and the aromatic mandarin trees.

FATHER ANTHIMOS, later called Saint Anthimos, was from the island of Chios. He was born on July 1, 1869, to pious parents. He had one brother who was called Nicholas and a sister who was named Kalliope. His sister later became a nun and received the name Kallinike at her tonsure to the Great Schema. Father Anthimos was not very educated. From his earliest years he was drawn towards monasticism, and this inclination led him to seek guidance from the Elder Pachomios, who was very renowned at that time and very virtuous. Saint Nectarios of Aegina had this same holy elder as his spiritual father. Letters written by Saint Nectarios bear witness to the great respect he had for Elder Pachomios and to his unswerving obedience to his spiritual guidance. On this same path towards sainthood, Father Anthimos lived under obedience to Elder Pachomios and was tonsured a monk by him. In 1910, Father Anthimos was ordained a priest.

Two years later he was assigned to serve the Leper Community of Chios. At that time, in 1912, the same year that the Turkish occupation of the island ended, the Leper Community was in a wretched condition. Out of his great love for these ailing people who were afflicted both in soul and body, Father Anthimos had soon brought about a total transformation to the place. He turned what had become a hellish enclosure for the condemned into an earthly paradise, full of shade-producing and fruit-bearing trees. He planted periwinkle vines, fragrant jasmine, and sweet violets. The institution's location itself was idyllic and the premises, rather than confinement, offered comfort. The entire complex consisted of 35 matching, little houses. Each of the little homes had a large room, a spacious kitchen with running water, a fireplace for heat, and other smaller rooms. There was also the Director's house, the pharmacy, and the refectory. In the middle of all these was situated a small, beautiful chapel dedicated to Saint Lazarus. Within the chapel was kept the wonder-working icon of the Mother of God, the "Panagia of Obedience."

THE ANCIENT ICON of the Mother of God, the "Panagia of Obedience," was discovered by Father Anthimos in a miraculous way, shortly after he became the priest of the Leper Community. The Most Holy Theotokos appeared to him in a vision and told him, "Take my icon and care for it diligently. One day you shall see what will happen here because of this icon." Indeed, after he plated the icon with gold and adorned it reverently, numerous miracles began to occur daily. This added even more to his reputation that had spread throughout all of Chios. Multitudes of the faithful were drawn to Father Anthimos like a magnet.

It was within this community of lepers and faithful that the most reverend Father Anthimos established his new protégé, the young Nicholas (soon to be Father Nikiforos). Eldress Bryene, the Abbess of the Holy Monastery of Panagia the Helper, recounted the following concerning this period: "There is something of interest in the history of Father Nikiforos that our holy elder once told us. The Leper Community required the large sum of 30 gold coins to accept the new patient since the institution normally accommodated only the lepers of Chios. And our saint, Father Anthimos, gladly gave this amount of money on behalf of young Nicholas. Originally, he had painstakingly gathered such a sum for the construction of the monastery. However, his gift was the only way the exception could be made for this foreign patient to be accepted at the Leper Community of Chios."

A portrait of Saint Nikiforos after his tonsure (by an iconographer
who was a leper at the Community of Chios)

A Monk Next to Saint Anthimos

In this new environment, the "arena of virtues" was opened wide for Nicholas. Within two short years, his elder, acknowledging his spiritual maturity and readiness to receive the holy Angelic Schema, tonsured him a monk. He gave him the name Nikiforos.

For 15 years, Saint Anthimos kept him continuously by his side, watching over him with fatherly care. He would counsel and advise him. By exhorting and encouraging him, he would lead him towards greater spiritual struggles, including vigils, fasting, and prayers. Saint Anthimos understood that he was dealing with good and fertile soil, and thus he kept on sowing spiritual seeds. Like an athletic coach, he would set contest after contest for his athlete—wrestling against the passions, thoughts, and demons—with the aim of acquiring the highest virtues.

The first fruit brought forth by Father Nikiforos' spiritual struggle was that his illness no longer stood in the forefront of his new life. His leprosy and all its ramifications took second place to the wonderful fruits of his new spiritual life. For certain the disease could not be forgotten. Regrettably, the leprosy was advancing and progressing, and in the absence of appropriate medications it caused severe damage. Yet despite this fact, the desire to ascend to the highest spiritual peak of sanctification now took primary importance in the life of the pious monk. Father Nikiforos was living for God.

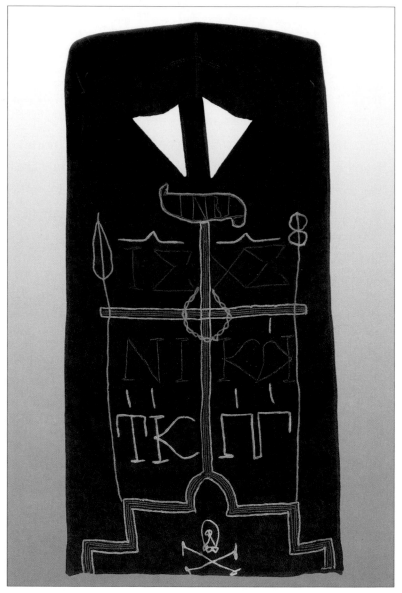

The monastic schema (habit) of our holy Father Nikiforos

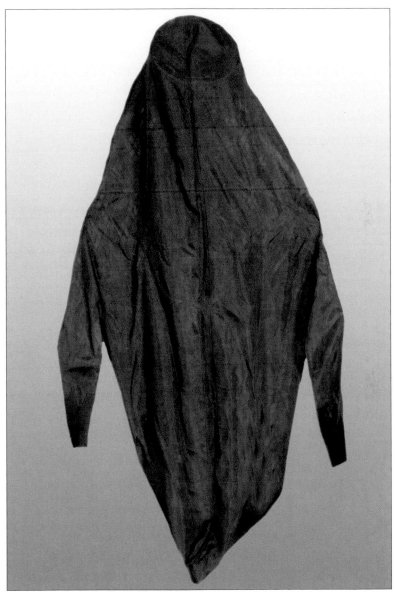

The koukoulion (monastic head covering) of our holy Father

He breathed Christ, he desired Christ, and he existed for Him alone. Every day, he was becoming more and more a God-bearing and Christ-bearing man. His obedience to his holy spiritual father was unquestioning, genuine, and perfect. He would even ask a blessing for the water he drank, as Eldress Bryene told us. His diet was strict, following the monastic tradition, always excluding meat and excluding foods cooked with oil on Mondays, Wednesdays and Fridays and during Great Lent. His spiritual struggle was that of a true monk, even though he was essentially living in a hospital and being treated with whatever medications could be found to relieve his tormented, leprous body.

Father Nikiforos always ate simple foods that had been prepared by the Community's cook. Having come to Chios as a refugee from Asia Minor, the cook had been healed of demonic possession by Saint Anthimos. She was a kind young woman and her healing was quite a remarkable event. Years earlier, her relatives had brought her to the church where Saint Anthimos was serving the Divine Liturgy. After the completion of the service, they laid her on the ground, while the demon inside her began shouting, "Everyone, get out!" Everyone left, except for Saint Anthimos and Father Nikiforos. She began to shout again, "Get Nikiforos out of here, too! Get Nikiforos out of here!" Saint Anthimos replied to her, "Let Nikiforos be. I want him here," and began to read the prayers for healing from demonic possession. Saint Anthimos then

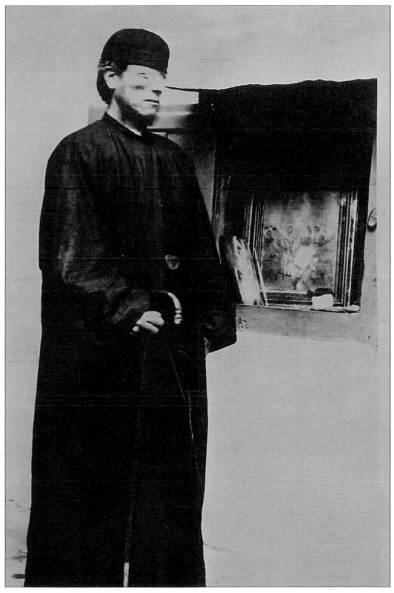

Saint Nikiforos, a monk in Chios

Saint Nikiforos with the young man Theodore in Chios

said to the demon, "Come out through her mouth."
"No," it replied. "Come out from her eyes." "No." "So,
are you going to come out of her nose?" he asked. "No."
"Well then, come out from her little finger." Finally, the
demon departed through the woman's little finger, which
immediately blistered and turned black. Once healed,
the young woman promised to remain and work there at
the Leper Community. Later, when it was shut down, she
became a nun at the Monastery of Panagia the Helper.
Father Nikiforos himself related this incident to his young
"disciple," Theodore Giannakis.

Little Theodore Giannakis—"Theodoraki" as Father
Nikiforos called him—was from Chios. When he was
just 10 years old, he was stricken with Hansen's disease,
and his parents brought him to the Leper Community.
The incurable leprosy forced the child to be separated
indefinitely from his mother and father, and confined
forever. Seeing the child's tragic plight, much like his
own, Father Nikiforos lovingly took the poor youngster
under his wing. Throughout the years that followed, he
would counsel and advise his precious Theodoraki. He
watched over him daily, and always comforted him with
fatherly love, concern, and affection. Little Theodore, in
turn, always listened attentively to Father Nikiforos. He
called him "Pappouli," which in Greek is an endearing
way to refer to a priest or monk. He deeply loved and
respected his dear Pappouli, like a true son loves and
respects his father.

Little by little, as Theodoraki became older, he also began to work together with Father Nikiforos. The institution allotted to each of the lepers a small piece of land where they could plant fruit trees and cultivate vegetable gardens. In addition to this beneficial occupation, many of the lepers also cultivated flowers as an exchange of love to the people outside of their community. They would grow the flowers in empty food cans to be sold at a local farmer's market. The ladies and housewives of Chios would come to the market especially to buy them. Truly, it was a paradoxical and poignant scene. Faces and hands disfigured and distorted by disease had prepared beautiful, fragrant, colorful plants and flowers of many varieties—jasmine, begonias, ferns, and more.

Father Nikiforos diligently cultivated many kinds of plants, just like the other lepers of the community. Towards the end of his time in Chios, however, the illness had adversely affected his eyes and he could not see well. He would say to his little Theodore, "Theodoraki, my boy, if I provide the property, will you do the work—plowing, watering, harvesting—and then we can share the crop?" This is the arrangement they made. With genuine self-sacrifice, Father Nikiforos, from the share of fruits and vegetables that fell to him, kept only a meager portion for himself. The rest they would load onto a little donkey and take to the beloved elder, Father Anthimos. In those latter years, Father Anthimos had taken up residence at the Monastery of Panagia the Helper, which he had built to accommodate many nuns.

> THE MONASTERY OF PANAGIA THE HELPER was completed in 1930. Saint Anthimos had begun to build the monastery in 1927 after encountering numerous difficulties and adversities. It was there that he established many nuns who had come from Asia Minor as refugees during the persecution of 1922. Up until the completion of the monastery, these nuns had been scattered across the island in different homes, receiving hospitality from the people. Many natives of Chios also went there to become monastics—truly blessed souls who wished to dedicate their lives to the Lord. Saint Anthimos himself also settled at the monastery after he resigned from his position as the priest of the Leper Community.

Saint Anthimos worked many miracles through the wonder-working icon of the Mother of God, the "Panagia of Obedience," throughout the years of his service to the lepers. Father Nikiforos was divinely enlightened to record these miracles, as the Athonite monk Theokletos of Dionysiou observes in his book, *Saint Anthimos of Chios*. He writes, "It would be an omission if we did not include here, in our narration of the life of the holy Father, the extensive catalog of those healed at the Leper Community, kept by the holy leprous monk, Nikiforos Tzanakakis, whom... [God] enlightened to record the miracles of the Mother of God, to the glory of God...."

Saint Nikiforos as a monk, together with his elder,
Saint Anthimos of Chios

The two saints with young members of the Leper Community of Chios

A LIST OF THESE MIRACLES was sent by Father Nikiforos to the Abbess of the Holy Monastery of Panagia the Helper in a letter from Athens, dated July 22, 1961. The following is an excerpt of what was written:

"I would like to inform you of some of the miracles of our most holy Father, as many as I remember. You should know however, reverend Abbess, that I came to the Leper Community of Chios in 1914. Our holy elder had come in 1912, so during those two years I do not know how many miracles he worked.

Here I am writing to you about those that I saw with my own eyes.

First there was a woman, now reposed, who had fourteen demons as the other demons testified. Thirteen of them left, but God allowed one demon to remain inside her, for her humility. Perhaps you remember how she would, at times, run to the fields and mountains. Especially while the Divine Liturgy was being served, the demon would try to choke her or throw her off a cliff.

Later, a young girl and her sister had demons, and he healed them; likewise another woman whose children are still alive. There was also a Cypriot who worked at the tannery, I don't remember his name—he was healed of demonic possession.

There was also a young priest who had come from Cyprus having a demon of pride, and he was healed. In remembrance of the miracle, he even left his pocket watch on which his name was inscribed.

After this, they brought a young man from Athens who was possessed by Beelzebub, the ruler of the demons, as he himself testified. He was healed. In fact, he even became a priest, finishing his life at a monastery.

Two brothers, both teachers, were healed from demonic possession.

Another man returned from England possessed and was healed, as was his cousin, who had embraced the monastic life. He also brought a girl who had set up a bird trap beside the river and blasphemed, and thus Satan found an opportunity to enter her; the demon would bark like a bulldog from inside of her. She was cured as well.

Then they brought another girl from a certain village and she was healed.

From the same village a woman came who was the sister of Father Ambrose, the abbot of the monastery of Myrsinidi; she had breast cancer and was healed.

They also brought another lady who had spent 300 gold coins on doctors that told her she had a neurological problem, but in fact she had a demon as a result of witchcraft; she too was healed.

A young child was completely blind, and he was made well.

In the city, in the house of a certain rich man, a great wrath had fallen. And what wrath? Each morning they would find all their kitchenware—big bottles, little bottles, glasses, vases, dishes—thrown in a heap in the middle of the house. They would put everything back in place, and then find it all in the middle of the house again the next morning. This continued for some time, until a certain pious person enlightened them, telling them, 'Go and bring the priest from the Leper Community. He is the only one capable of helping your situation, since he has boldness before God, as we see from his countless miracles. Bring him to your house so he can pray to God to stop this wrath.' So it happened that our holy elder went to the house, prayed to God, and the wrath ceased. I don't remember now the name of the householder.

Another time a man who was a senator of Chios and member of Parliament became ill and was on the verge of death. His son-in-law was a doctor. Neither he nor the other doctors of the region were able to find the cause of his illness. His daughter, however, the doctor's wife, had great faith and respect towards our holy elder. She urged her husband to send for our holy elder, to bring him to the house, and so he did. Upon his arrival, he heard the weeping and wailing of the family and many others who were present. As soon as he approached them, he said, 'Don't cry. He will become well, and tomorrow he will return to his office.' Perhaps some of them scoffed at him. He approached the man, blessed him with the sign of the Cross, blew on his face, and—what a miracle!—that very moment, he fully recovered and was restored to health. From that time on, the doctor admired him and held him in high esteem. Indeed, he was able to help the elder when the authorities wanted to imprison him for the healings he performed; it was he, after God, that freed him from their charges.

Once, they brought an 18-year-old girl and she died just outside the premises of the Leper Community. They had brought her to our holy elder to get healed, but unfortunately they did not come in time. Nonetheless, they begged our holy elder to bury her in our cemetery. He granted their petition, and they buried her in our cemetery. After three years, our holy elder went to the cemetery and opened the girl's grave. He saw that her whole body had decomposed except for her right hand, which remained completely without decay. She had even stretched it out as someone does when cursing another with a hand gesture. The nails of her hand had continued to grow. Immediately her relatives were notified to come without delay. When they arrived, he asked them, 'What did this girl do that caused her right hand not to decompose?' They told him the only thing they could think of: 'She had had an argument with our village priest, and as soon as the priest turned his back to leave, the girl turned towards him and cast a derogatory hand gesture. That is all we know.' After they told him this, our holy elder went to the cemetery and knelt beside her grave for three days, praying for God to dissolve her hand. And—what a miracle!—on the third day her hand had turned to dirt.

In all this that I have written, I am informing you of what I know and what my eyes have seen. Later on, if I remember anything else, I will write to you. But I would have you know, reverend Abbess, that he possessed the gifts of foresight and prophecy, and he knew the future, as he often revealed to me. He did not want these gifts to be made known, so as to avoid worldly glory.

With spiritual love,
The lowly monk, Nikiforos Tzanakakis"

The book, *Saint Anthimos of Chios*, elaborating on this special bond between Saint Anthimos and Father Nikiforos, relates the following: "During the divine services, the purity of [Saint Anthimos'] holy soul shone forth on his sacred face, and when he served the Liturgy he would see divine light coming down upon the Holy Gifts. This he confided to the monk Nikiforos, who remained inseparable from him at every step during all the years of his service at the Leper Community. Not a single thing that the elder did escaped his notice."

Saint
Anthimos,
the elder
and spiritual
father of
Saint Nikiforos

A MIRACULOUS AND CHARMING NARRATIVE, further exemplifying the holiness of Father Anthimos, was related by Father Nikiforos himself to one of his close acquaintances. Once upon a time, there was a mouse in the church that would climb up and eat the wicks of the candles and oil lamps. One of the lepers, Sotiris, who would light the candles, became very upset with the situation and informed the elder, Father Anthimos. "Don't worry, Sotiris," the elder replied. "Panagia will catch the thief." The next day, on June 24ᵗʰ, the Divine Liturgy was to be served in commemoration of the Nativity of the Holy Forerunner, John the Baptist. Everyone who had gathered in the church that morning beheld in front of them the mouse climbing up onto a candle in the candle stand. When it reached the wick, the mouse was suddenly suspended in the air by some invisible force. It was still holding the candlewick in its mouth when Sotiris ran to the scene and began trying to burn the mouse with a lit candle. Yet even though the mouse was clearly being burned and suffering much pain, it remained immobile. At that moment, the elder came out of the Holy Altar to cense the church during the 9ᵗʰ Ode of the Matins service, which specifically honors the Panagia. Looking towards the candle stand with a smile, he said to the poor animal, "All right, you've had enough. Come down now." Immediately, the invisible bond was loosed, and the mouse jumped over and sat on the elder's right shoulder. The elder picked it up and said to it, "If you enjoyed that, come

The entrance to the church of Saint Lazarus at the
Leper Community of Chios

Little houses of the Leper Community of Chios

back again to eat some more wicks!" Then he tossed it out of the church. From that day forth, not a single mouse was ever seen in the church, nor anywhere within the premises of the Leper Community.

Each of the little houses of the institution typically accommodated two or three people living together. Father Nikiforos, however, lived alone as a monk. At night he would pray for hours on end. He would make countless prostrations. The leprous monk persevered in these ascetic struggles until his hands and feet had become so deformed by the illness that he was no longer able. These details of Father Nikiforos' personal life and struggle were recounted after his repose by his little "disciple" Theodoraki who also related the amazing account that his beloved Father Nikiforos had never quarreled with anyone. With his limitless humility and love for others, he had never made another person sad.

From his earliest years in the village of Sirikari, Father Nikiforos had always attended regularly the services of the church. At the Leper Community in Chios, he would ring the bell of Saint Lazarus' church every evening. Many of the lepers would gather, and they would read the Compline service with the Salutations to our Panagia. Every morning, with the help of a nun who was also ill, Father Nikiforos would chant the Matins service. On Sundays and feast days, he was the main chanter of the church. The Metropolitan of Chios, Panteleimon Fostinis of blessed memory, once heard him chant and remarked,

"That monk chants like an angel." A nun from the Holy Monastery of Panagia the Helper also remembered Father Nikiforos' chanting. She narrated the following: "Once, when Father Nikiforos visited our monastery and was in the narthex of the church together with Saint Anthimos, he was asked to chant the hymn to the Mother of God, 'It is truly right to bless you.' When the nuns heard him chanting, they gathered in the narthex whispering to one another: 'What an angelic voice!' But when the saint lifted his head and they saw the sores on his face, they were dumbfounded."

This earthly angel bore yet another burden on account of his illness: gradually he lost his sight. For this reason, he sang most of the hymns from memory and recited the Epistles by heart. Needless to say, the loss of his physical eyes made everyday life very difficult for Father Nikiforos. And yet, as a result of this physical hardship, his spiritual life became something incomparably loftier and more beautiful. The eyes of his soul were opened, and he was enjoying spiritual visions and contemplations. These are "the eyes with which angels also see, eyes that see God," as Saint Anthony once said to Didymos.

> SAINT ANTHONY THE GREAT once went down to Alexandria where he met with the well-known director of the Theological School, Didymos, who, though blind from childhood, was one of the wisest men of his time. Saint Anthony told him: "Don't let it bother

you in the least, Didymos, that you lost your physical eyesight, because with such eyes the flies and the mosquitoes also see. Rather, be glad, because you have the eyes that angels see with, eyes that see God and perceive His light."

It was behind these gates that Saint Nikiforos lived for 43 years in Chios.

An interior view
of the church
of the Holy
Unmercenaries
at Saint Barbara's
Hospital in Athens

His Last Years In Athens

In 1957, the Leper Community of Chios closed, and the remaining patients, among whom was Father Nikiforos, were sent to the Leprosy Treatment Center of Saint Barbara in Athens.

THE LEPROSY TREATMENT CENTER of Saint Barbara is a sizable facility stretching across several acres in Aegaleo, a western suburb of Athens. At that time, the Treatment Center had many pine trees, vines, and fruit trees. It consisted of four large buildings, three of which were built during the administration of Theodore Pangalos to accommodate the soldiers who were there for military target practice. These buildings were located on the northern side of the existing Hospital for Infectious Diseases, which was established in the year 1900 when epidemics of the plague, cholera, and especially smallpox were scourging the population. The buildings were converted into rooms for patients suffering from Hansen's disease. There were also small houses where one or two patients, or small families of lepers, would live together.

A LARGE CHURCH was built to serve the needs of the patients from their own contribution of their meager savings. The church, dedicated to the Holy and Glorious Unmercenary Healers, is functional to this day and attracts multitudes of people. Yet, there was a time when no one would dare to set foot there for fear of being contaminated. Only a few sympathetic and courageous souls would lay aside all fear in order to bring a little joy and comfort to the pained and wounded brethren who lived there.

In 1957, when the lepers from Chios were transferred, Father Sophronios Saridakis (later Father Evmenios), an ailing monk, lived at the Treatment Center. Saint Anthimos advised him in a closed letter he had sent to be delivered by Father Nikiforos himself: "Take good care of this treasure Panagia has sent you. From his life you will derive much benefit for your own life, for he is not only a tried and tested monk, but also a perfect monk. You, too, will become perfect if you serve him until the end of your life."

When Father Nikiforos came to Athens, he was 67 years old. His arms and legs, indeed all the blessed members of his body, had become completely deformed and disfigured from the illness. Over 50 years of suffering from leprosy had completely deteriorated his eyes and his vision, and spared no portion of his holy, suffering body. Because he was so severely disabled, Father Evmenios, in his boundless compassion, took care for his every need with great zeal and love.

FATHER EVMENIOS, whose secular name was Constantine Saridakis, was born on January 1, 1931 in the village of Aethia in the region of Herakleion, Crete. He was the eighth and youngest child of a large, poor family. In 1948, when he was only 17 years old, he left behind the secular world and its affairs and went to live in the monastery of Saint Niketas in southern Crete. In 1951 he was tonsured a monk and received the name Sophronios. A few years later, while serving his time in the military (in those days, even monks were required to serve in the military), he was stricken with Hansen's disease. He was admitted to the Leprosy Treatment Center of Saint Barbara, and due to a prompt diagnosis and successful treatment he was completely cured. The disease did not leave even a single mark on his body, unlike the miserable case of Father Nikiforos. Nonetheless, he decided to live the rest of his life at the Leprosy Treatment Center alongside his ailing brethren. He would care for them in every way possible with much love.

In 1975 he was ordained to the priesthood by Archbishop Timothy of Crete and received the name Evmenios. From that time, in his capacity as priest, he comforted and consoled many souls from Athens, all of Greece, and even from abroad, receiving them at the Treatment Center's Chapel of the Holy Unmercenaries or in his little cell. He was an exemplary Liturgist who tirelessly celebrated the divine services with majestic solemnity and exactitude. As a confessor, he was discerning, insightful and fatherly. Many hastened to him for confession—lay people, monastics, priests, and even bishops. His spiritual life was characterized by unceasing inner prayer of the heart, obedience, and fasting hidden from the eyes of men; he was truly a man of great spiritual struggle. In his relations with

Father Evmenios

others he was lenient, courteous and gracious, never critical, always smiling, affectionate, and very charitable. He departed to the Lord on Sunday, May 23, 1999, leaving behind the reputation of a great and holy man. His life was virtue and virtue was his life. Truly, in him the saying of Saint Isidore of Pelusium found complete fulfillment, "He acquired the nature of virtue, which cannot be touched by death."

With true love and sacrifice, Father Evmenios served Father Nikiforos and cared for all his needs. He cooked his simple food daily and gently fed him his small portions. He bathed him regularly and dressed him, and with every attention to detail, he would even take time to tenderly clean his ears. One day when he was putting Father Nikiforos' shoes on, he applied a little too much pressure. This slight movement caused pain in his feet, which were very sensitive. All his toes had essentially been worn away by the illness. Pappouli told him, "You hurt me, my child." Father Evmenios, overcome with grief, leaned forward on Father Nikiforos' chest and pleaded with him saying, "Forgive me, Pappouli. My dear Pappouli, forgive me." The reverence, love and respect that Father Evmenios nurtured in his heart for his blessed Pappouli were truly exemplary.

Father Nikiforos himself was in no manner demanding, despite his extreme physical disabilities and needs. He manifested a character and personality quite the opposite of what one would expect from someone in such an ailing condition. He displayed only extreme meekness, humility, and submission, and avoided imposing on anyone for any reason. He dedicated himself to unceasing prayer, enduring his terrible situation patiently and with joy. As a reward for his patience, the Lord granted him many spiritual gifts, one of which was the gift of comforting the afflicted.

A multitude of people flocked to Pappouli. Strangers completely unknown to him—suffering from sorrow, pain, depression or despair—began to visit him in order to find comfort and consolation. Well-known people of society would run to him to receive his blessing and counsel. Among them were the ever-memorable Dionysios, Metropolitan of Lemnos, later of Trikkis and Stagon; Nikiforos, Metropolitan of Lefkas and Ithaca; Efthymios, Metropolitan of Acheloos; the ever-memorable Metropolitans Leonidas of Thessaloniki and Nicholas of Chalkis; the former abbot of the Holy Monastery of Dionysiou on Mount Athos, Archimandrite Gabriel of blessed memory; Father Elias Mastrogiannopoulos and many others.

More than any of those who came to see Pappouli, it was his fellow patients in the Treatment Center who found the utmost shelter, fatherly love and affection in his saintly person. Next to him, they regained the hopefulness and optimism that were so easily lost in their daily struggle with sickness and anguish. His small hospital room, his humble little cell, became a place of daily pilgrimage, a true spiritual "pool of Siloam." One of his visitors wrote how "his fellow patients always found in his presence the 'gladsome light.' And even his visitors who were healthy in body received health of soul from the strength and vigor of his own soul and spiritual life."

In the midst of his community and despite his many visitors, the main work of Father Nikiforos remained spiritual watchfulness. Both in company and solitude, he would occupy himself with unceasing noetic prayer. It was this prayer that he knew well and in his ascetic strivings he had truly mastered it. He had been taught to pray this way by his spiritual father, Saint Anthimos, who had been taught by his own elder, Pachomios, the spiritual father of Saint Nectarios. Father Nikiforos, in turn, handed down this prayer to his spiritual child, Father Evmenios, who had been waiting many years to find someone who could teach him the Jesus Prayer.

A spiritual child of Father Evmenios, Bishop Neophytos of Morphou, related the following in regards to this beautiful succession: "Father Evmenios became a monk at the Holy Monastery of Saint Niketas on the island of Crete. However, he was called for military service, during which time he fell ill and ended up at the Leprosy Treatment Center of Athens. He remained there as a monk and later a priest, but he had not lived in the monastery for many years so as to experience the monastic life in depth. For this reason, while living and struggling alone at the Treatment Center in Athens, he often wondered whether or not he was living his monastic life correctly. Day and night he would beg our Lord and our Lady the Theotokos to reveal to him an enlightened and grace-filled person who could teach him about prayer. It was precisely then that Father Nikiforos came from Chios, bearing a letter from Saint Anthimos that said, 'Take care of this treasure, this priceless pearl....' Father Nikiforos was indeed a rare and priceless pearl, well versed in noetic prayer and a worthy teacher. From that time on, Father Evmenios turned to him as his spiritual father and guide, until Pappouli fell asleep in the Lord."

The Athonite monk, Father Gervasios of blessed memory (†November 2000), from the Holy Monastery of Simonopetra, recalled: "Around 1960, I went with a group of fellow students to visit Saint Barbara's Hospital for Infectious Diseases in Aegaleo. At that time, very few people would visit the Leprosy Treatment Center. We found there a very sweet, venerable elder, Father Nikiforos—a grace-filled, God-bearing and virtuous man. After we took his blessing and sat down, he asked us, 'My children, do you pray? And how do you pray?' We told him that we pray with some spontaneous prayers, as we learned at gatherings we attended. He said to us, 'Not that way. Pray with the Jesus prayer, "Lord Jesus Christ, have mercy on me." This is how you should pray. This is the right way.' And slowly, little by little, he taught us the Jesus prayer."

Father Gervasios concluded, "We went to visit the lepers in order to console them, and they taught us how to pray."

A man who had contracted leprosy at the young age of 13, recalled, "I would visit Pappouli's cell, and for however long I stayed I saw that he was praying. He would move his fingers in the way that we pray with the prayer rope."

Saint Nikiforos in his last years, in his little cell at Saint Barbara's Hospital for Infectious Diseases in Athens

His Repose

On January 4, 1964, at the age of 74, our most venerable Father Nikiforos surrendered his soul into the hands
of the Lord. His funeral was held on the following day,
the Eve of Theophany, in the Treatment Center's church
of the Holy Unmercenaries. Many of the other patients,
along with his friends and visitors, were in attendance.
He was buried in the small cemetery designated for the
lepers, next to the church. His funeral was a mystical
experience. It created a profound awareness of the sanc-
tity present in the ancient Orthodox faith from the time
of the early Church. Everyone was convinced of Father
Nikiforos' holiness and there was an undisputed sense
that not just an ordinary person was being buried, but a
saint.

When his relics were exhumed, they were found to be
fragrant. In accordance with the saint's desire, the relics
came into the possession of his spiritual child, Father
Evmenios, who kept them with much reverence in a small
chest inside his room. He used to say, "I have my Pappouli
here; he's right here." He would bring out the little chest
with the holy relics, which exuded an ineffable fragrance,
and would cense them often. In this way he continued to
manifest the great respect, deep reverence, and boundless love that he fostered towards his spiritual father.

The book, *Saint Anthimos of Chios*, describes the holiness of Father Nikiforos with these words:

"But before we present the record of those healed, we deem it necessary to say a few words about the one who wrote this record [i.e. Father Nikiforos], in order to emphasize its credibility.

When this blessed leper fell asleep in the Lord in 1964 and passed on to the bosom of Abraham like another Lazarus, religious periodicals published eulogistic obituaries, one of which said the following:

THE SAINT OF THE LEPERS

Holiness was living in the Leprosy Treatment Center of Saint Barbara's Hospital in Athens. During the first week of the New Year, that holiness departed for the New Life, for eternity.

Father Nikiforos Tzanakakis spent many, many years inside the poorest of cells, unknown to the world, but well known among the angels and saints.

He was a penniless monk, a leper, blind, and practically paralyzed. Yet his eyes, although they had lost their light, beamed with ascetic holiness, and the divine smile never faded from his trembling lips until his last breath....

The monk Nikiforos, the spiritual offshoot of the venerable Elder Anthimos Vayianos of Chios, was a bright page in the book of Christ's church, despite his incredible obscurity...."

... Nikiforos the Leper, during the darkness of his long and painful trial, had received from the All-Holy Spirit the gift of clairvoyance.

To this day I continue to seek his prayers and intercessions.

Metropolitan Efthymios of Acheloos

TESTIMONIES

TESTIMONY OF HIS EMINENCE METROPOLITAN EFTHYMIOS OF ACHELOOS

hroughout the decade of 1955-1965 I served as the General Secretary for the "Worldwide Fellowship of Orthodox Youth SYNDESMOS." The year that I was a deacon (1962-1963) I visited Saint Barbara's Hospital for Infectious Diseases and served during the Divine Liturgy.

After the Divine Liturgy I was brought to a small room, the dwelling of the monk Nikiforos. He was a leper, both blind and bedridden. I did not know him nor did he know me. It was the first and only time we met.

We began a spiritual conversation without any hesitation. It made an impression on me that this monk, who was a leper and blind, took part with such interest and liveliness in the discussion. In fact, he was the one who did most of the talking. I can also remember how our lengthy spiritual conversation did not seem to tire him at all.

During our conversation I was especially struck by the following incident: Because of my position as the General Secretary for the Fellowship SYNDESMOS I was in correspondence with the Ecumenical Patriarch Athenagoras, as well as with other patriarchs, hierarchs and dignitaries of the Orthodox Church. This matter did not come up during our conversation but perhaps Father Nikiforos had been informed of my position—that I do not know.

At one point, completely spontaneously, the leprous monk expressed the following thought:

"Some clergy even imagine that they will become Patriarchs!"

These words spoken by the monk greatly perplexed me—it was as if he had read my mind. I had this exact, persistent thought. Although I do not remember what had given rise to it, the thought was creeping like a worm inside of me at that time.

The incident caused me to believe that Nikiforos the Leper, during the darkness of his long and painful trial, had received from the All-Holy Spirit the gift of clairvoyance.

To this day I continue to seek his prayers and intercessions.

September 17, 2002

TESTIMONY OF ARCHIMANDRITE NIKODEMOS GIANNAKOPOULOS:
FATHER NIKIFOROS, SPIRITUAL STRUGGLER AND GUIDE

I met Father Nikiforos in 1961 at the Hospital for Infectious Diseases, which was still known then as the "Leprosy Treatment Center." I went together with a youth group led by the former Deacon, now Metropolitan of Chalkis, Nicholas Selentis. He encouraged us to bring some joy to our ailing brethren who were rejected by society and isolated—to embrace them, to eat together with them from the same plate, to receive Holy Communion after them.

One of these "outcasts" was Father Nikiforos. The marks of the illness were obvious over his entire body: he was blind, maimed and disfigured, and had no physical strength. Nonetheless, everyone who visited him immediately sensed that radiating from inside this ailing body was a spiritual strength, a godly zeal, a boundless love, and a peace that permeated one's entire being.

That which I still remember vividly is how he would struggle against the demons. They attacked him often, sometimes even physically, but he would bring them into subjection with the power of the Cross. He scourged them with the name of Jesus, and compelled them to confess their demonic activities. "Tell me, scoundrel," he would say, "Where were you last night?" And if the demon confessed that someone had defeated him, Father Nikiforos would rejoice and give glory to God; but if it told him that a Christian soul had fallen into his snares, he would grieve and pray.

His little hospital room was for us a place of spiritual help and joy. We had before us a struggler who "fought the good fight," and we received strength from him. His fiery prayers had boldness before the throne of God, and they conferred on us the refreshing dew of the Holy Spirit. He would draw us up toward his own spiritual height and inspire in us divine zeal. Unfortunately, in my own case, this zeal would quickly fade.

In his great simplicity, without complex teachings, he provided spiritual guidance. His life itself was a teaching. He revealed God to everyone, for even when he was silent God was speaking from within him. "For it is not you who speak, but the Spirit of your Father who speaks in you." (Matthew 10:20)

May we have his blessing, and may he intercede for us, that we find mercy on the Day of Judgment.

Various Short Testimonies

 Someone wrote of Father Nikiforos: "The spirit of the Lord rested on this individual."

Another wrote: "His eyes, although they had lost their light, beamed with ascetic holiness. The divine smile never faded from his trembling lips until his last breath. It was a smile from heaven that shone upon the leprosy of our modern times."

Bishop Nikiforos of Lefkas and Ithaca said: "When I would visit his little cell during the early 60's, I would see him rejoicing with all his soul, as if he were seeing Christ before him, above him. He was a very spiritual man."

Elder Maximos from the Cell of the Entrance of the Theotokos in Kerasia of Mount Athos related: "From what I remember, Father Nikiforos was a man of great patience and endurance, a model for us of the spiritual life, a hidden saint."

One woman related that in 1957 Father Nikiforos came to the Treatment Center. They put him near Father Evmenios, who was still called Father Sophronios at that time. "Father Evmenios made Father Nikiforos his spiritual father and lived under obedience to him. Back then, Father Evmenios used to eat meat; they imposed it on him as a patient of the Treatment Center. But when Father Nikiforos came, who did not eat meat, Father

Evmenios stopped eating meat also. They would each read the services on their own; Father Nikiforos knew them by heart. He didn't pray with the prayer rope because he was physically unable to do so. He died in 1964, the day before the Eve of Theophany."

Theodore Giannakis (Father Nikiforos' little "disciple" Theodoraki from Chios) relates: "I left Chios on June 1, 1950, and came here [to the Leprosy Treatment Center of Saint Barbara]. The Elder came later, in 1957. They had also brought the rest of the lepers from Chios, but for me, it was Father Nikiforos who had captured my love and my sympathy. He was my consolation. I would go and sit with him in his room. His blessings and his counsels were an invaluable treasure for the rest of my life. He was truly worthy to be loved."

A patient of the Treatment Center, a man of great virtue who has now reposed, narrated: "I would often visit Pappouli's little cell because being near him comforted me a great deal. Even though he was blind, almost paralyzed, full of sores and in pain, he never complained and never grumbled; rather he would comfort and console the rest of us. He was very sweet, gentle, and always smiling."

Mr. John Spyropoulos remembers: "I met the ever-memorable monk, Father Nikiforos Tzanakakis, 50 years ago when I visited the small Leper Community of Saint Lazarus in Chios. His image is imprinted indelibly in my memory. He was of average height, lean because of his ascetic way of life, with a gaunt face and a beard that was sparse because of his illness; he had sunken cheeks with protruding cheekbones, and yet his expression was soft, joyful and smiling. His eyes were always tearing and irritated, and his vision minimal. His leprosy made the joints in his hands stiff and rigid and caused paralysis in his lower limbs. Despite all this, he was a joyful person, pleasant to be around, and he had a keen sense of humor. He spoke with a distinctive and high-pitched voice. On the feast day of the Panagia I attended the service at the church of Saint Lazarus, the community's small chapel. The chanter at the right choir was Father George, a priest ill with leprosy, and at the left choir, Father Nikiforos. His minimal vision and his deformed, stiff fingers made it difficult for him to turn the pages of the books and read the hymns written in them. This, however, did not hinder him from serving as a chanter because he had learned almost everything by heart. His voice may not have been as beautiful as Metropolitan Panteleimon Fostinis made it out to be in his book, *Myrrh-flowing Chios*. However, he sang with passion and he hymned our Lady the Theotokos with all his heart. Once in a while his chanting would bellow out like thunder if someone in the congregation were talking too loud or wandering around inside the small chapel during the Liturgy. Father Nikiforos ate together with us at the festal meal in the afternoon. His face shone with cheerfulness as he enjoyed the company of his fellow-diners, and—as he loved joking—he would tell innocent jokes to the great delight of the whole group.... In Athens at Saint Barbara's hospital, I visited him only on a few occasions; one of those was in the company of the former Archimandrite Nikiforos Dedousis (today Metropolitan of Lefkas)."

A man from Patras narrated: "I visited the Leprosy Treatment Center of Athens very often to see Father Nikiforos because I was always comforted by his presence. This Pappouli must have had the gift of foresight. Whenever I would knock on the door of his cell, before I had a chance to identify myself, he would call from inside, 'Welcome, Constantine!' One must bear in mind that by this time Pappouli had completely lost his physical eyesight. He had told me that one time when his disciple, Father Sophronios, was very ill, he began to pray for him fervently, both day and night, day and night. This irritated the demons and they attacked him severely, to the point that he was fighting against them physically, pushing them away with his poor crippled hands."

Another man recalls from his visits to Father Nikiforos: "We witnessed a saint whose face shone brightly, conveying joy, peace and calm, and we gained strength from a seemingly weak man."

One woman related: "Whenever my husband would go to the village to plant our fields, he would first go to receive the blessing of Father Nikiforos. Our crop was always so bountiful that it made an impression on the owners of the adjacent fields, and they would ask us, 'How are your fields producing so much? What are you doing differently than us?' My husband would look at me with a knowing glance and say, 'Do you see what the blessing of our Pappouli does, and how much power his prayers have?' Also, Father Nikiforos used to tell us, 'My children, you should pray so that Satan won't harass you, because he is harassing the whole world.'"

Another woman, also a patient at the Leprosy Treatment Center, described how Father Evmenios would look after Father Nikiforos who was a monk. His eyes were damaged by leprosy and he could not see well. His feet were shriveled up and so were his hands. Father Evmenios would care for him, cover him, and give him food and water.

One day when Father Evmenios went to Father Nikiforos' little cell, he found him praying and he saw his face bathed in light. In his prayer, he was harshly accusing himself. And he told Father Evmenios, "My child, when you pray, accuse yourself."

One man writes: "It was in 1963 when the leader of our Christian Youth Group announced to us that we would attend the next service of the Salutations of the Theotokos all together at the church in Saint Barbara's Hospital for Infectious Diseases.

Early Friday afternoon we all met in New Ionia, eight to ten junior high school students, together with our youth director who had arranged this opportunity for us to combine the Lenten worship service with a charitable visit of love.

After the service we saw and spoke with many people, patients and visitors at the Treatment Center, because our youth director was a regular visitor there and knew many of them well. Afterwards he brought us to receive the blessing of Father Nikiforos. He had previously spoken to us about him at our gatherings, describing his struggles, his patience, his trials, and his holiness.

We visited him in his poor but blessed little room. He was sitting on his bed, covered with an army blanket. Standing next to him was Father Evmenios, ready and eager to serve him.

Father Nikiforos' face shone with joy, even though both his face and hands were covered with sores from his illness. He did not have a beard but only a few sparse hairs. He must have also had a problem with his eyes because he was wearing dark glasses. Even his voice was weak and distorted.

He was very glad that we came to visit him, and he gave us his blessing and fatherly counsels. At one point he also described to us how he fought with Satan. His disciple, Father Evmenios, rolled up Father Nikiforos' sleeve, showing us the scratches the demons had left on the elderly man's feeble arm. Father Nikiforos then told us that only prayer and the sign of the Cross make the devil leave, trembling and defeated. 'Because you are young and wish to lead a Christian life,' he told us, 'he will fight you. You, however, must not be afraid, because with the power of the Cross you can chase him far away.' We thanked him and took his blessing, and on our way home we discussed our impressions.

Many years have passed since then, but that child-hood experience of our visit to the hospital and the holy elder remains forever indelible in my memory.

Since then, his counsel concerning the value and power of prayer has remained not only in our thoughts, but also in our hearts and on our lips. Many are the trials and temptations of life. The words of Elder Nikiforos, however, were and are a 'Niki-foros' (literally, 'victory-bearing' in Greek) example in our life. May we always have his blessing."

Kontakion. Tone 4.
On this day you have appeared.
Next to God who honored you,
O Nikiforos,
you do stand with boldness now,
like the tenth leper who returned,
in great thanksgiving and gratefulness;
so as is fitting, we honor your memory.

(Written by Archpriest Stylianos Makris)

Testimony of Elder Justus

(Of the Kathisma of Saint Nicholas, Karyes, Mount Athos)

I was not even 20 years old when the youth directors of the Apostle Paul Youth Group at the School of Engineering arranged our first visit to what was then known as the "Leprosy Treatment Center" of Saint Barbara in Attica.

On Sunday, after attending the church of Saint Spyridon in Piraeus, we gathered the packages we had prepared to bring to the Leprosy Treatment Center. I was very apprehensive, wondering what sort of people we would meet there, because until then I did not even know what it meant for someone to have leprosy.

When we arrived, we passed an entrance that was under the strict surveillance of gatekeepers. One of the guards, a young man, led us to the priest who was in the church. It was there that I first encountered those who suffered from this horrendous illness. My gaze was fixed on the little children and on the young men and women. I freely shook hands with any of the sick people who offered their hand to greet me. The elderly man who was in charge of our group gave me some magazines to hold and whispered to me, "You don't need to shake hands with them. Just talk to them."

We had organized a small celebration for the children. After we gave them their gifts, before we left the church, the elderly leader of our group turned to me and asked me to say a few words to those who were ailing. Full of emotion, and with much reservation, I managed to say something to them, and kept reiterating the following wish: "The next time we come here, I hope that you all will have recovered and returned to your homes and your families."

As soon as we had departed from the premises of the Leprosy Treatment Center, the elderly man in our company turned and said to me, "You blundering idiot—what were you saying to them?"

"What did I say, Mr. K.?"

"You fool—these people will never recover. The disease is incurable."

I was thunderstruck. I could not believe that these people would never get well. With trembling lips I asked, "Those little children? And those 14-year-olds? They will spend their whole life sick in this place?"

The elderly man became very serious. "Yes," he replied, "they are here until they die. You didn't know that?"

"No...no... I can't accept that... that's injustice... it's a sin... something has to be done for those young children!"

Their faces, all eaten up by the disease, had left me horrified.

I do not even remember how I made it home. In any event, it must have been past the hour when we would eat lunch all together, because as soon as my mother saw me she asked, "Where were you, mister, and why are you home so late?" She began to scrutinize me, and then the interrogation began:

"You look troubled. What's wrong with you?"

"Nothing."

"That's not true. I gave birth to you and I can tell when something is on your mind. Speak to me."

"Nothing is wrong with me. I'm just very sad. We went to the Leprosy Treatment Center at Saint Barbara's and...."

My mother interrupted:

"Inside or outside?"

"Inside. We brought some things for the patients."

"Get out! Out of the house! Go out in the yard! I'll bring you the rubbing alcohol and a change of clothes. What are you, crazy, my child, to go catch that accursed disease that's worse than tuberculosis?"

After I was "disinfected," she called me to the dining room to eat. When I told her that I was not hungry, she looked me straight in the eyes and said, "Listen my child. I know you very well. You shouldn't be going to such places because afterwards you'll keep thinking about it. But what can I do, now that you've got yourself involved in those Christian organizations—all they do is take you to those sorts of places."

I visited the Leprosy Treatment Center a few more times with the other leaders of our organization in order to entertain the children and bring things to them.

Two of the older members of the group would visit a certain monk who was in a graver condition; they would not allow us younger ones to visit him. But all the while that I kept company with the children, my thoughts would continually wander to the monk of whose virtue everyone spoke so highly.

The years that followed were full of school and work. Then I was called for military service; I left Attica and stopped visiting the Leprosy Treatment Center.

Meanwhile, good news was spreading. The French academic Raoul Follereau had launched a great crusade on behalf of those suffering from "Hansen's disease" (as "leprosy" was renamed). The "Leprosy Treatment Center" became known as the "Hospital for Infectious Diseases."

I felt that a wound had opened in my soul from that very first day I set eyes on those ailing children and heard about the ill monk. I was never able to erase them from my memory and my soul. I was 30 years old when I crossed the threshold of the Hospital for Infectious Diseases once again.

An archimandrite with whom I was acquainted had recommended that I go to meet a certain bed-ridden monk named Father Nikiforos. This was the same monk I had heard of years earlier when I visited with the youth leaders from our school. And so I went to visit him one Sunday afternoon. I found him alone, lying in a dark room that was rather like a prison cell.

The little bit of light that shone from the window lit his somehow darkened face. I leaned over to kiss his hand, but he did not allow me to. "It's not necessary," he said, indicating for me to sit in an old chair that looked like those you used to find in coffee shops.

With very few words, he asked me about myself— what job I had, if I was married, who my spiritual father was, etc. I responded to him somewhat at length in order to establish a comfortable atmosphere. At the same time, I was speaking with reserve and respect, for I was persuaded that the man in front of me was no ordinary person.

I had my head bent down a little at first, but when I looked up I saw that he was looking me straight in the eyes. I took courage and began to look him in the eyes as well; otherwise I did not want to stare at his face, covered with sores from his illness, so that he would not think that I was scrutinizing him out of curiosity.

Looking at him, I sensed that behind those eyes there existed a long life story, full of struggle, patience, fortitude and expectation. They were neither joyful, nor were they hopeless. They did not exude bitterness, but they did express a silent and reserved grievance that emerged from the depths of his soul.

At one point he told me, "You are young, and your voice is very passionate. Be careful in your life. More valuable than any pleasure or enjoyment is the peace of your soul. I do not have your temptations, but for many years now I have faced the trials and temptations of illness. Glory to You, O God. God knows why He allows temptations."

By this time I was altogether staring at him in awe and did not want him to stop talking. From his gaze I felt a deep certainty that within this tormented monk Christ was truly alive.

He crossed his arms over his chest and said a few words in prayer very softly, barely audible. The sight of him captivated me, even though the sparse hairs of his beard were not enough to conceal the leprous wounds on his face.

He looked me straight in the eyes and said, "The time has passed and it's almost dark. Go with God. I thank you for coming to see me."

I wanted to kiss his hand, but again he did not allow me to do so.

When I walked out I felt stronger, but I also had a lump in my throat. I needed to cry. I restrained myself and murmured through clenched teeth, "Why, my God, is this holy man so harshly tormented? Why?..."

I cannot even remember all the numerous times I directed my steps towards him after that first encounter. Whenever I would think about him, hear his name, or hear something about the development of his illness, I felt as if someone in my own family were suffering. I lived with my thoughts in that dark little room they had allocated to him, small and mournful—even his covers were dark like army blankets. The only bright object in the room was an icon of the Panagia, which seemed to be the only wellspring of hope there, both for the permanent resident and for anyone who visited him.

Intentionally or not, your glance would shift between the pained face of the monk and the holy icon, and without even thinking about it your soul would fervently entreat the Mother of God, the great Intercessor for those in pain. At times, a vast silence would prevail. We both understood the gravity of his illness and were each immersed in our own thoughts. Then, with a faint smile appearing on his face, he would say, "May His holy Name be glorified." He would say this right before I departed; it was as if he wanted me to leave without any sadness or worry. I would bid him farewell, saying, "I will come again, Father Nikiforos."

Whenever I left, I felt as if I were leaving a piece of myself there in that dark cell, which was illumined by a monk whose life was a furnace of trials and afflictions and who was waiting for the day when God would bring him out into refreshment (cf. Psalm 66:12 [LXX 65:12]).

Thirty-eight years have passed from that day when God gave him rest from the tribulations of this world. My thoughts often turn to that little "Job." I close my eyes and try to envision him before me, as he was that first time I met him in his dark cell when he stressed to me to be careful and live according to the will of God.

Now, O blessed Nikiforos, I have grown old, and perhaps soon I shall pass over to the life that has no end. I beg you, pray that I be numbered among the Lord's faithful servants who show true repentance.

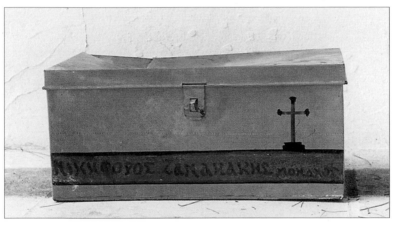

The original small chest that contained the fragrant holy relics of our God-bearing Father Nikiforos

MIRACLES

ather Evmenios related how he would attend to Father Nikiforos, put him to bed, and then go to his own cell to rest. One evening, Father Evmenios was unable to sleep. He had a troublesome feeling that perhaps he had forgotten to do something for Father Nikiforos. He thought, "Maybe the wood stove was not closed properly." This and other such disturbing thoughts were troubling his mind.

Becoming more and more restless, he finally got up and went to Pappouli's little cell. In order not to disturb him if he were already sleeping, Father Evmenios did not knock on the door, neither did he say, "Through the prayers of our holy fathers, Lord Jesus Christ our God, have mercy on us," and wait to hear the response, "Amen," as is the custom among monastics before entering another's cell. Instead, he opened the door slowly and quietly. And what did he behold? Father Nikiforos was hovering about a meter off the ground, with his hands raised in prayer and his face shining more brightly than the sun.

As soon as he caught a glimpse of this truly awesome and fearful sight, Father Evmenios, without saying a word, closed the door very carefully and ran back to his cell. There he fell to the ground, and with his face on the floor, began weeping and sighing. He greatly feared that he might have grieved or distressed his Pappouli when he had opened the door without knocking and seen him in that miraculous state. He also wept from joy, because he had witnessed with his own eyes the greatness and virtue of his spiritual father. In the morning, when Father Evmenios went to care for him as usual, he made a full prostration to the ground before Father Nikiforos and asked forgiveness for his offence. The saint, with a gentle smile, forgave him immediately and told him not to reveal to anyone what he had seen until after his death.

F ather Evmenios also narrated the following occurrence, which took place many years after the repose of Father Nikiforos. One evening, because his cell was full of mosquitoes and various insects, he decided to shut the doors and window and empty a whole bottle of potent insecticide in the room. Without a second thought, he lay down to sleep. But he would never have woken up had Father Nikiforos not appeared to him, waking him and leading him by the hand out of his cell. Before Father Evmenios completely understood what had happened, Father Nikiforos told him, "My child, don't go back into your cell without opening the doors and the window so it can air out well," and immediately he disappeared.

After some time, Father Evmenios came to himself. He understood the miracle that had occurred, and with all his heart he thanked Father Nikiforos—his beloved Pappouli—for saving him from certain death.

Hieromonk Amphilochios from the monastery of Saint Paraskeve in the city of Megara related that as he was sitting in his cell one day he began to smell a fragrance. He searched high and low but could not find the source of the aroma, which in the meantime was intensifying. Finally his eyes fell on a large, thick, postal "security" envelope. He opened it and found inside a piece of holy relics that exuded an ineffable fragrance, together with a small note, "Father Nikiforos Tzanakakis, January 4, 1964."

These holy relics belonged to another hieromonk who sent them to the monastery temporarily for safekeeping while he was traveling. Only when Father Amphilochios removed them from the envelope and reverently placed them together with other holy relics did the fragrance become a little less intense.

The Athonite monk Father Kallinikos related: "When I was given a small piece of the holy relics of Father Nikiforos, it was fragrant. Later, however, the fragrance went away. One day when I went to venerate the relics, I said to Pappouli, 'My saint, I am not worthy, but I beg of you, be gracious to me and do not turn away from me the sinner.' Then—what a miracle!—the relics became fragrant once more. After a few days when I went to venerate them again, as soon as I opened the little box that held the holy relics, my entire cell was filled with an ineffable aroma. I was immediately inspired to write the following Megalynarion to the saint: *Having suffered many adversities, you resembled, Father, by your patience, the righteous Job. As a living icon of virtue, you have pleased God; thus after death, sweet fragrance comes from your relics now.*"

Hieromonk Matthew related that when Hieromonk Epiphanios came to serve as the priest for the church at the Leprosy Treatment Center after the repose of Father Evmenios, he found in a chest some of the relics of Father Nikiforos. Father Matthew made a request of him, saying, "I would like you to give a piece of the sacred holy relics to me as well." And Father Epiphanios replied, "I will bring it to you personally the next time I come to Thessaloniki."

Indeed, after a short time he brought a piece of the relics. They placed them inside a little box on top of a table and lit a candle beside them. Shortly thereafter, another priest came to visit Father Matthew. He saw the relics, venerated them, and asked, "Who is that saint whose relics are so fragrant?" "I didn't believe him at first," Father Matthew confessed, "but when we went to venerate them again, truly they were fragrant. As time passed, the aroma increased. This lasted for many days. I have venerated the relics of many saints, but this was the first time I experienced something so remarkable."

A clergyman who was harassed by lawsuits for many years and whose case had reached the Areopagus (Supreme Court of Greece) said: "In October of 2003, before my court hearing, I called on Father Nikiforos to help me. And truly, Pappouli helped me. The public prosecutor sought my acquittal, and I was declared innocent."

Theodore Giannakis (Saint Nikiforos' "Theodoraki") narrated the following miraculous event:

"In the 90's I was facing a serious lawsuit. They had involved me in some affair and I was being asked to pay an enormous sum of tens of millions of drachmas. The initial court hearing had condemned me, but when the matter came to the court of appeal, I asked Father Evmenios to give me a piece of the relics of Father

Nikiforos that were in his possession. 'Father,' I told him, 'I cared for Father Nikiforos. I washed him, I dressed him, I cooked for him, I cleaned his dear little ears, and now that I am in great need I want him to help me.'

He gave me two small pieces of the holy relics. I received them with much reverence, embracing and kissing them. I kept them with me during the trial. Before it began, I said a prayer within myself, fervently begging Pappouli to help me during this difficult time. And—what a miracle!—the public prosecutor put forth that I was not guilty, and the court declared me innocent. I thank my Pappouli from the bottom of my heart for helping me again, just as he used to, even though many years have passed since his repose."

A man from Athens related the following:
"In June of 2002, one night, or rather towards dawn, I saw in my sleep that I was in a house with two rooms. In one room was Pappouli, Father Nikiforos, and I was in the other. I was in my room talking to someone, loudly and intensely. After a while I entered Pappouli's room and said with joy, 'Good morning, my dear Pappouli.' I went to the corner of the room where he was lying and leaned over respectfully to kiss his hand.

He turned to me and said in a fatherly voice that was quiet but very clear, 'My child, because you have ulcerative colitis, you must be more calm, more peaceful. Have you noticed that your health is better in the winter? It is because you are calmer then.' I thought to myself, 'How clearly Pappouli is speaking today.' After a little while, I saw him get up and go outside, where he sat down in a little electric wheelchair and sped off. He left me with the splint that he was wearing on one of his legs.

It is worth noting that in one of the rooms of my house where I pray I have a portion of his relics, which exude an ineffable fragrance. When I awoke, I called my spiritual father and told him what I had seen in my sleep. He told me, 'Truly it was Pappouli who appeared to you to advise you concerning your chronic illness, because of the great love and respect you have for him.' Indeed, it is well known that doctors recommend peace and quiet to people who suffer from this condition—both of which I lack completely."

The same man narrated the following:

"In August of 2002 I was on Mount Athos at the Skete of Saint Anne. I was staying at the Kyriakon. In the morning I attended church at the cemetery of the Skete.

During the course of the service, a layman arrived and came uninvited to the chanter's stand where I was chanting. He began to chant very slowly, with lengthy intonations and extensive pauses, completely disregarding the tempo and rhythm we were keeping before he came.

At some point I told him that the daily services on the Holy Mountain are chanted at a faster pace. He paid no attention to me, as if he were in his own world. I started to get very upset and soon I was boiling with rage. My nerves had been stretched to their limits.

At that very moment, I remembered the advice of Father Nikiforos. 'My Pappouli,' I prayed, 'my dear Pappouli, help me. As you see, I am unable to restrain myself and calm down on my own. Please help me.' Then, without even realizing it, I calmed down and became peaceful. I followed the Divine Liturgy with great compunction. You would never have imagined that my episodes of nervous exasperation usually lasted for many hours, or even days.

I have related these things to the glory of God, of our Lord Jesus Christ, and of His servant our holy Father Nikiforos."

A pious young Christian visited Father Evmenios one day and said to him, "Father, I heard that you have holy relics of your spiritual father, Father Nikiforos. I would like to have a portion as a blessing, to protect my family."

Father Evmenios gave him a piece of the relics, which he reverently wrapped and placed in his shirt pocket (it was summer) and then he returned home on his motorcycle.

As he was returning home, even though he was driving very quickly, he continually sensed an ineffable fragrance. Despite the fact that the aroma naturally should have been taken by the wind at the speed he was traveling, as he himself attested, this fragrance was completely inundating him.

Even more significant, however, was the following occurrence: When he arrived at home, he called out to his wife, "Come quickly to venerate the holy relics I brought." His wife came to venerate them, but jumped back in alarm shouting, "It burned me! It burned me!" She later affirmed, "When my lips came close to the holy relics, I felt an intense warmth, something like a burning. It scared me so much that I jumped back."

From that time on, his wife's faith greatly increased. Up until then she was more or less indifferent to spiritual matters. Together, they placed the holy relics in their prayer corner with their icons. They keep a vigil lamp constantly lit before them.

Upon hearing that the life of Saint Nikiforos the Leper was being prepared for publishing, a lady from Thessaloniki made a spontaneous offer, saying, "I would also like to help cover the costs of publishing."

It is noteworthy that she knew nothing about Pappouli, nor had she ever even heard of him. Because a significant amount of money was required for the publication, she sent her contributions in increments every so often.

At one point, she neglected to make her contribution in a timely manner. As she relates, it was then that she started repeatedly seeing along the roadside signs with the name, "Nikiforos," "Nikiforos," and thought to herself, "It has been a long time since I sent money for Pappouli's book."

She immediately went to the bank and sent a sum of money, then returned to her family's business. That day, no customers had come by and her father announced, "Since we have no work here, I am going to leave." Having said his piece, he left.

Immediately thereafter, so many customers began to come that the personnel did not have time to serve them all. Within a few hours, their profits were more than double the sum that had been sent for the publication. "Is that not a miracle?" she concluded. "First, that I repeatedly saw the name 'Nikiforos,' 'Nikiforos,' and then for our business to suddenly reach an all-time peak?"

Another time, the same lady related: "One day, when I was somewhere between sleeping and waking, I saw a venerable elder coming towards me. When he had come rather close to me, he said, 'I am Nikiforos, the Pappouli. I came to tell you to be careful, because there are people who wish to harm you, to do something bad to you.' Pappouli continued, 'And listen, my child. I want you to be the sponsor of my icon.' As soon as he said this to me, he disappeared. Truly, I do have some relatives who wish to do me harm. If possible, they would run me out of business."

A third miraculous event occurred regarding the same lady: Before Pappouli's book was completed, she called Father Simon[1] one day and said, "Yesterday I was at my home in Panorama of Thessaloniki. As I was leafing through a book, I remembered Father Nikiforos, and it was as if I heard a voice telling me, 'the icon, the icon.' The next day I went and deposited a sum of money for the publication of Pappouli's book, to which I had pledged assistance."

Father Simon told her that if she had called a little earlier, he would have notified her to send a portion of her donation directly to the Holy Monastery of Xenophon on Mount Athos where the icon had been commissioned. In fact, the iconographer, Father Luke, had already completed and delivered the icon of Father Nikiforos. "That's all

---

[1] Father Simon is the author of the Greek edition of this book about Saint Nikiforos. Prior to its publication the saint was essentially unknown.

right, Father," she replied. "In a few days I will be able to collect more money and send it to him."

Ten minutes later she called back, saying, "As soon as we got off the phone, my father handed me an envelope, saying, 'This is for you.' I opened it and found exactly the amount of money needed for the icon—neither more nor less. I was speechless. As soon as I recovered from the shock I picked up the phone to call you and relate to you this miraculous occurrence."

Another man from Athens related that many times when he attended services at the church of the Holy Unmercenaries he would suffer from headaches. In great pain, he would go to the room where the little box with Father Nikiforos' holy relics was kept. As soon as he would make the sign of the Cross over himself with the relics, the headache would go away.

Once, when Father Evmenios was very sad and was sitting alone in his cell, he saw the door open by itself. In walked Father Nikiforos who had reposed many years before. As Father Evmenios himself narrated: "He came and stood next to me and said, 'Come now, my blessed child, don't cry, don't be miserable,' and he patted me on the head. The more he caressed my head, the more I felt a breeze. It was the breeze of the Holy Spirit, and it kept increasing until I was completely, entirely filled with this breath, this breeze that emanated from the caress of his hand. My distress disappeared."

Metropolitan Neophytos of Morphou

August 3, 2005

My venerable father and my elder, Simon,
Rejoice in the Lord, and may the grace of our Lord Jesus Christ be with you always.

I am full of joy, my elder, that a bright new star has appeared in the heavenly firmament over the dark world in which we live, and with its divine rays of light has illumined my pained soul.

There was a certain time when I was earnestly praying to find a holy person or some book to encourage me even a little. I went to the bookstore of the Apostolic Ministry of the Church of Greece and searched all the shelves, but did not find anything that interested me. I was very sad, but as I was getting ready to leave I thought to myself, "Let me just take one last look and then I will leave." At that very moment I saw in front of me this excellent book. Without the slightest hesitation, without even opening it, I purchased it. Within 45 minutes I had read the whole thing and I was delighted by the life of the ascetic martyr. I say "martyr" because the sickness he endured was a martyrdom. Taking hope in his divine

help and protection, I called you immediately and was very glad to speak with you who are so familiar with the grace and divine protection of the ascetic martyr.

I hope and anticipate that the intercessions of the holy ascetic martyr Nikiforos the Leper will mediate for us before the divine and heavenly Altar.

I send this letter to you with prayers and blessings.

Pray for me, the thrice-wretched and sinful priest.

Father Athanasios Regalos
Piraeus

Once, when I was in a very difficult position due to my many economic obligations, I went to the bank to take out a loan for 50,000 euros.

I was disappointed, however, when they informed me a few days later that I was approved for only 45,000 euros, instead of 50,000, for reasons of low tax disclosure. And this was decided despite the fact that there was a guarantor.

I told the bank employee, "Thank you very much, I do not want the money, it does not meet my needs. You can close the transaction."

When I returned home in distress, I kneeled down and begged Saint Nikiforos, our Pappouli, to help me. Moreover, I told him, "My good Pappouli, do not reject me, the sinner. Help me through this difficulty."

The next day, around noontime, they called me from the bank again and said, word for word, "Father, come take out your loan. The sum you requested was approved after all. It seems that miracles happen for you priests."

The intervention of Saint Nikiforos in this situation was indisputable. Through his intercessions, my request was granted. I thank him from the bottom of my heart, and beg him also to intercede before the throne of God for me, the sinner.

P.S. It is noteworthy that I have read the book about Father Nikiforos eight times.

Father Methodios Capeliaris
The Holy Metropolis of Megara and Salamis

By the grace of God, I was ordained to the priesthood on December 12th, the day our Church honors the memory of Saint Spyridon the Wonderworker. Praying together with us in the holy altar during the course of the Divine Liturgy was our beloved brother, the monk Father Simon of the Holy Mountain. After the service, together with his warm wishes, he gave me a little envelope. "A small blessing," he told me.

That same day in the afternoon, when I found some time free from visits and phone calls, I began to open the various gifts I had received, among which was the envelope with the "small blessing" from Father Simon. Inside were two beautiful, small prayer ropes and a small laminated icon of our holy Father Nikiforos the Leper—the same icon which is printed on the cover of his biography—in which was sealed a tiny portion of his holy relics, about the size of a pin head.

Because Father Simon had spoken to me about Saint Nikiforos, I had read his life and developed a special reverence for him. Hence, I felt immediately that this was no "small blessing," but rather an enormous one. I thought it fitting to place the icon with the relics on the holy altar table of the small chapel in my house where I would be serving Liturgy for 40 days after my ordination, as is tradition.

During these Divine Liturgies our holy Father revealed his grace and his presence to us, the lowly ones. Ineffable fragrance that often intensified wafted from the icon, filling the altar and usually the whole church as well. Witnesses of this were the chanters and everyone who attended and prayed at the services, who in the beginning wondered, "What beautiful incense is this?"—even at times when the censer was not lit.

These incidences of fragrance have continued to occur, consoling us, supporting us and giving us courage in our struggle so that we might continually exclaim, "Wondrous is God in His saints."

Archimandrite Hieromonk Gregory

March 4, 2005

F ather Simon,
    I read something about Elder Nikiforos in the life of Saint Anthimos of Chios, but had not given it much attention. The other day when I went to the bookstore, *The Garden of the Panagia*, I saw Elder Nikiforos' book. I was drawn by the beautiful icon on the cover and read a little about Pappouli's miracles and the fragrance of his holy relics. I ended up leaving without buying the book because I was suffering tremendously from a headache. Riding on the bus on my way home, I just randomly had the thought, "Father Nikiforos, if you are a saint, take away my headache." By the time I arrived home my troublesome headache was gone.

Although I did not think much of it at first, I believe this was a sign from Pappouli. Later, when I read the whole book and learned of Pappouli's other signs, I realized that this was yet another one of his miracles.

I await your response, and if you can, I would like you to send me something from Pappouli—a small icon, and (if possible) a small piece, even just a sliver, of his relics.

Bless!!

P.J.
Seminarian at the Graduate Theological
School of Thessaloniki

Today, February 16, 2006, after my morning prayers, I greeted my saint, Pappouli Nikiforos, and set off for work. After I opened my business, I decided to go to the salon and get my hair cut. While I was there, one of my employees called and told me to return to the shop because an auditing agency had come.

I left immediately as I was, with wet hair, so that I could be present at the audit. The officials of the agency, very strict and exacting people, took a very long time and I started to get cold—very cold.

The day was such that despite the sun there was a biting chill. I began to feel unwell. With all the strength of my soul I said to my Pappouli, "Saint Nikiforos, you must come here."

At that moment exactly, the officials of the auditing agency got up and prepared to leave. "We finished the audit," they said, and they bid us farewell and left. I remained dumbstruck for a minute because for me this was a miracle. I ran inside to put on something warm and felt much better. While I was cold, I did not feel well. I was pushing myself. I called on Pappouli and he came and protected me. To me, Father Nikiforos is a great saint.

P.S. It is my great blessing and treasure to have a piece of his holy relics in the chapel at my home.

C.G.

Herakleion, Crete

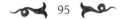

On the morning of January 29, 2005, I prayed as usual to Saint Nikiforos and asked for his help and protection throughout the day. I have him as my personal guardian, and every day I ask him to shelter me and protect me from all trials and temptations. That day, after my prayer, I started to get ready to go to work but kept encountering minor delays. For example, shortly before I left home, my dress ripped and I had to go fix it. As soon as I mended it, it ripped again and I had to repair it once more.

When I finally set out to leave, I took out the garbage with me but as soon as I set foot outside, the bag ripped and the garbage spilled. I went back inside to bring another bag to replace it.

I cleaned up the mess and set out to leave once more, but had barely taken two steps when the garbage bag ripped open again, the garbage spilled on the ground, and again I had to go inside to find another bag.

By this time, I began to feel that something was keeping me from leaving home—it was as if someone was delaying me on purpose. I finally managed to set out for work, but as soon as I got on the highway I encountered unbelievable traffic. The cars were not moving at all in any direction.

I was completely blocked in and there was no way to get off the road. Meanwhile, I was running low on gasoline, and if these circumstances continued any longer I would confront another serious problem. I decided to call the highway patrol and inquire what exactly was happening.

I was informed that a very serious accident had taken place on the highway a short distance ahead of me, but they did not know how long it would be until the road opened.

In my anxiety I picked up Saint Nikiforos' book, which I always keep with me in the car. I began to call upon him, asking him to open the road.

Sure enough, as I was entreating the saint, traffic began to move and slowly return to its normal flow. After I proceeded a little on the road, I realized that there were even fatalities in this major accident. One car had swerved trying to avoid a dog that had jumped out into the road, and all the cars behind had crashed in a terrible multi-car collision.

What is amazing about this is that it had all happened at exactly the time I would have been driving at that point on the road, had I not been delayed in leaving that morning.

It was then that I understood what a great miracle Saint Nikiforos had worked for me. He saved me by ensuring that I was not on the road at the specific time and place the accident occurred. The saint heard my supplication in the morning for protection and help, and it was he who kept me from leaving home on time.

M.V.
Thessaloniki

O ne day while at home, my mother sensed an intense fragrance permeating the house. At first it seemed to her as if someone had censed the house with some sort of extraordinary incense.

She began to look around the house to find the source of this heavenly scent. She opened all the doors and windows to see if perhaps the fragrance was coming from outside, but did not discover anything. Eventually she came to a certain place in the house where Saint Nikiforos' book was kept, and there she sensed the fragrance very strongly.

She experienced this fragrance three times. Then she began making the sign of the Cross, kissing the saint's icon, and thanking him for his visit that day, which gave her strength and consolation in the trials she was undergoing at the time.

M.V.
Thessaloniki

January 4, 2006

R everend Father Simon,
I read over and over again the book that God blessed you to write about the life of Saint Nikiforos the Leper. I was moved by his humble and pure character, his patience and uncomplaining stance towards the afflictions he bore on account of his illness (which was incurable in

those years), his love for the Lord, and his wholehearted dedication to prayer.

Thus I was inspired to direct my pleas to him and seek his intercession for a serious problem that I was encountering in my work environment at that time: my supervisor had begun to hold an unprecedented negative stance towards me, insulting me, slandering me, and completely defaming both my person and my work (which I avow that I carried out in all good conscience, with all eagerness and efficiency).

I continued to call upon the intercessions of Saint Nikiforos the Leper and his alone, believing that if the miracle were to occur and my supervisor were to change his attitude towards me, it would necessarily be a result of Saint Nikiforos' prayers, as I did not call upon the intercessions of any other saint. I would thus be able to testify with a letter concerning the persuasive intercessions of the saint before God.

Several months later, I returned to my office after a few days' vacation. I was informed that my supervisor had assigned me to a very responsible position and put me in charge of a matter that presupposed his faith in my person and abilities. Shortly thereafter he called me on the phone and spoke to me in a serious but very friendly tone of voice. He publicly commended my systematic method of work in front of my co-workers, and expressed his personal interest in increasing my resources for my new work.

Everyone who knew the supervisor's former attitude towards me was astonished at this truly miraculous change. I glorify God for His saint, Nikiforos the Leper, calling upon him more and more often, and with faith and fervor I advise others to become acquainted with him.

With gratitude, to the glory of God,

P.D.

May 29, 2006

In the fall of 2005, I was visited by a court magistrate, summoning me to two court cases on the same day. One was regarding the alimony that I was supposed to be receiving for my child (which I still do not receive). The other was concerning the demand of my former husband for custody of the child, in which he used words that insulted my character.

The evening before the court date, I prayed a great deal. I set the icon of Saint Nikiforos in front of me and begged him to help me and quickly deliver me from this ordeal. That night, I saw the saint in a dream and he was looking at me. I understood from this that I would surely have his help.

The next day, at the first trial, I did not stop praying the entire time. The only words I heard were those of the judges, spoken strongly against the father, and moreover, sentencing him to prison for seven months. At the second trial, he did not appear at all—nor did his lawyer—and the case was closed.

I understood that I, too, have a "protector" and "guardian" in the person of Saint Nikiforos, to whom I am so grateful and love with all the strength of my soul.

E.P.
Athens

June 3, 2006

I read the biography of Saint Nikiforos the Leper and was touched by the great toil, patience, faith, and endurance that you describe in the newly revealed saint. At first, I read it meticulously several times over, and now, every so often, I read it again. I am always inspired by the struggles of this new Job.

I would like to relate to you two events:

1) On my way to work I pass through Moschato of Attica, where I would always see an elderly woman accompanied by three dogs. At first, I never paid much attention to her. One day, however, I asked myself, "You, who are always so obsessed with your work, have you ever looked around to see whether there is someone truly poor and needy and perhaps have passed them by?" Sure enough, the next day, I saw the little old grandma rummaging in the garbage, together with her dogs. I realized that she kept the dogs for company. I love dogs also, so I had two reasons to approach her.

She told me that she had a bad back and that she had no one to help her collect the benefits to which she was entitled. I remembered how I had reproached myself about not seeing people in need and I offered to help her.

We went to the social service doctors (this was the procedure), but the psychiatrist there had previously stopped the elderly lady from getting her benefits, demanding that she first go to the public psychiatric hospital for examination and assessment. But little grandma insistently refused to go there because she believed that if she entered she would never come out again—such a fate had befallen some of her acquaintances.

Seeing this challenge, I decided to seek help from Saint Nikiforos the Leper. To really begin the proceedings to secure grandma's benefits, we would need to go to the Social Security office of Kallithea. At that time I was living in my country home in Anabysso of Attica. I made sure that I had Saint Nikiforos' photograph in my wallet. I kept praying, seeking the aid of the saint in this matter.

I got into a taxi with little grandma and we proceeded to the Social Security office. I was holding a plastic bag with all of her papers. When we got out of the taxi, I forgot the bag with the papers in the back seat. I quickly realized this, but in the meantime the taxi had left with another passenger. I was very distressed; in that bag were all of the woman's documents—her ID cards, health records, etc. I stood in a daze there where the taxi had left us, in the afternoon sun.

Another taxi driver next to us who was watching the whole scene, when he understood what had happened, said to me, "*Eli, Eli, lama sabachthani.*" These words struck me like a knife, but I did not open my mouth. Little grandma kept telling me, "That's OK, Mr. George. It doesn't matter if I don't get my benefits. I'm all right, people take care of me."

I took hold of my wallet with the picture inside and said, "Saint Nikiforos, didn't I ask you to help me? What am I going to do now? How am I going to help little grandma with her affairs?" All the while, however, I had faith inside me and I waited there. "God will do something," I said to myself. "I'm going to wait."

Less than ten minutes later, the taxi driver came speeding back; he stopped and gave me the bag. "Saint Nikiforos is with us," I said. "We may have a hard time, but everything will turn out well." And that is just what happened. The people at the Social Security office were understanding of the problem, and today little grandma receives her benefits.

2) My second experience with Saint Nikiforos was as follows: For some time, I had a strong desire to practice the Jesus prayer. I understood, however, that without a guide either I would not make any progress, or else I would progress in the wrong direction. The one option was bad and the other worse. And so I kept searching for a guide.

When I read that Saint Nikiforos had a deep knowledge of the prayer, it stuck in my mind. From then on, it was as if I were waiting for some instruction from him.

One morning before dawn, around 5:00 or 5:30, as I was sleeping on my right side, I somehow felt or saw spiritually that Saint Nikiforos was next to me. He grabbed one of my hands and then the other and raised me up so that I was sitting on the bed with my feet resting on the floor. There he left me. I felt rested and joyful, like a little bird. I understood that he was instructing me to get up (and in general, to wake up early in the morning) and to say the prayer sitting like that. Thus I sat there and prayed for quite some time.

These are my two experiences with Saint Nikiforos the Leper.

With much love and thanks,

G.K.
Professor of Economics, Athens

One day I received a book about Saint Nikiforos the Leper from Father Simon. It made a deep impression on me and I felt a great desire to get to know the saint.

For two weeks I begged Saint Nikiforos to make me worthy to get to know him and to pray to him with fervor, through the prayers of his disciple Elder Evmenios.

After two weeks, one evening in my sleep I found

myself in a village in the region of Eurytania, in the house of Father Simon's father (I must add that I have never visited Father Simon's house).

His brother Theophanes was waiting for me there and told me, "Come on, little one, hurry up, I want to introduce you to the Elder." In the corner of a beautiful room I saw a bedridden, venerable elder who stretched out his hand and blessed me with the sign of the Cross. I awoke with great joy. The next day I looked at the picture in the book Father Simon had sent me, and recognized the same face I had seen in my sleep.

I thank the Lord that He allowed me, through the prayers of Elder Evmenios, to meet Saint Nikiforos.

Nun Photini

September 19, 2005

A woman from Herakleion, Crete, lives with her bedridden mother and her brother who is also ill. She is 60 years old. She relates, "I purchased the book of Saint Nikiforos the Leper, and while I was reading it I sensed a fragrance spreading across the room. Around 11 o'clock that night, as I was going towards my brother's room, I smelled the same fragrance in the hallway of the house.

I smelled this delicate fragrance three times, and I thanked the saint because I was so moved by his presence.

I believe that he granted this in order to comfort and strengthen me, since I live with two people who are ill. He was ill, too, and he knows about these things."

February 8, 2005

A man from Peristeri wanted to visit Mount Athos but could not get leave from his work at the County. Because he had recently read the life of Saint Nikiforos, he spent a whole day begging for the saint's assistance in this matter. In the evening he saw the saint in his sleep, exactly the way that he looks in his icon. "Don't worry, my child," he told him, "I'm going to help you."

When he went to work the next day, they informed him that he would be given 10 days vacation, even though they had formerly ruled out any such possibility. The man went to the Holy Mountain for a week, and when he returned he called Father Simon in tears, informing him of what Saint Nikiforos had done for him, "the sinful and unworthy one."

January 8, 2005

Another woman from Herakleion, Crete, related that she had a very serious problem. She called on Saint Nikiforos and her problem was resolved in the best way possible.

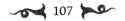

A woman from Volos has a 12-year-old daughter named Stella-Constantina. "On March 5, 2005," she said, "I purchased the book, *Nikiforos the Leper*, but did not read it right away. The next day my daughter picked up the book to read it, and as soon as she opened it she smelled a fragrance. She called me saying, 'Mom, the book is fragrant! The book is fragrant!' I went near to smell it but did not perceive any fragrance. My daughter, however, continued to smell it. Who knows? Perhaps because she is young and innocent, that is why she is the only one who smells the fragrance."

November 10, 2006

Reverend Elder, Bless.

I am writing this letter to inform you of something that happened to me seven months ago that relates to our most holy and ascetic father Nikiforos the Leper, whose biography you wrote.

Initially, I would like to mention that I first learned of the saint from a presentation of your book in the magazine, *Families with Many Children*, which sparked in me a desire to find the book and read it.

This desire of mine was fulfilled during Bright Week of 2006, when I went on a pilgrimage to the Holy Monastery of Saint Nectarios in Aegina with my family. I found and purchased the book at the monastery's bookstore, and finished reading it before I returned home to Volos.

I was greatly moved and, instinctively, my heart filled with love and marvel for the "glorious athlete of endurance."[2] Words of supplication to the saint spontaneously began to pour forth from my lips. I entreated his assistance because, for about a month, I had been having trouble with my right thumb. It was constantly numb and occasionally it would cause me intense pain. I made the sign of the Cross over my thumb many times with the icons of the saint that are printed in your book, begging him to show his sympathy to me, the insignificant one, and to relieve me of this problem through his prayers.

After all this, as we returned to Volos, I felt a deep inner assurance that the saint would answer my pleas, despite the fact that my thumb was bothering me intensely that day. Indeed, by the time we reached home I began to feel better. By that Sunday, Saint Thomas Sunday, it was completely healed and has not bothered me since.

I firmly believe that the grace of God, through the prayers of our wonder-working ascetic father, Nikiforos the Leper, worked this miracle for me, the sinner and lowly one, as a sign and as an opportunity for repentance.

And so I write you this letter to inform you of this

---

[2] This was the subtitle of the original Greek edition of Saint Nikiforos' book.

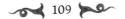

incident, to the glory of God and the honor of our won-der-working ascetic father Nikiforos.

With respect,

A.Z.

Professor of Theology, Volos

October 2006

In July of 2006, I had gone to Rome with some friends of mine to see the catacombs and other significant sites. As we were returning home, we encountered a major problem at the airport. Even though we arrived on time, when we went to check in, we were informed that the flight to Athens was full and we would not be able to travel. Another 10 or 15 people were told this as well. We were taken by surprise. I was in a difficult position, because I had already secured a ticket to travel to an island the next morning. We did not know what to do so we shouted and pleaded. I explained that I was a police officer and needed to leave because I had another flight to catch the next morning, but completely in vain. One of my companions had with him a small icon of Saint Nikiforos the Leper with a little sliver of his holy relics. He took out the icon, we venerated it, and we begged the saint very fervently to help us in this difficult moment.

Shortly thereafter, one of the airline's managers, who in the beginning was as negative towards us as everyone else, suddenly changed his attitude. He came, took our tick-ets, went into the company's office, and after a while sent another employee to take us to the departure gate. There, we found panic and upheaval as about 40 people from Paris were supposed to board the same plane. Just then, the manager of the airline came out, took us to the front of the line, and told the employees who were making the last check for boarding, "These are my friends, and they are going on this flight."

And so we departed from Rome. After boarding the airplane, we realized the direct intervention of the saint and thanked him from the bottom of our hearts.

I wrote this short letter out of gratitude to the saint, and to the glory of God, and once again I thank the saint wholeheartedly.

A.K.

Theologian, Elatochori, Pieria

A woman from Carpenisi related: When I was pregnant with my second child, my husband and I thought about naming him Nikiforos if he were a boy, because we were so moved by the book we read about the life of Saint Nikiforos that was circulating at the time.

We did not reveal this thought of ours to anyone. Some time had passed when I received a phone call from my older sister (I am one of four sisters; three of us are married and have children) who told me, "When your baby is born, you shouldn't name him after our father, because our other sister already gave his name to her son." "What name do you think we should give him?" I asked. "You should call him

Nikiforos," she told me, "after that saint who was a leper, the one we read about in that book that was just published."

When I heard that, the telephone almost fell out of my hands. I was so touched that we both had the same thought without ever having discussed it. Furthermore, I was glad because the fact that we both had the same thought seemed to mean it must be pleasing to the saint. I believe that my son will be the first to be named after Saint Nikiforos the Leper. May we have his blessing.

June 2007

Last year I had experienced a great miracle of Saint Nikiforos the Leper at the airport in Rome, Italy. But that was not the end of the story. When I recently went on a pilgrimage to Constantinople, I experienced another great miracle of the saint.

We were setting out to return to Greece when, in the lobby of our hotel, I noticed that my passport was missing. After looking through all my belongings, I concluded that I must have lost it. We were supposed to fly in three hours and I had no passport.

This was going to cause problems: I would have to stay longer in Constantinople and would also lose my ticket. My fellow pilgrims and I tried to work out how we would still be able to leave within three hours and not lose our flight.

At the same time, we were all praying to Saint Nikiforos to help us. And indeed he did. Even though in

Constantinople they were observing Ramadan and everything was closed, with the help of the saint we found a photographer's shop open. We took the pictures that the Consulate would need to give us paperwork confirming the loss of my passport.

The Consulate itself was also closed for the holiday, but with much effort we were able to find the responsible secretary who helped us quickly and willingly. Even our taxi driver served us with self-denial, speeding, making U-turns, and turning into one-way streets.

Halfway to the airport, however, we realized that in our haste and anxiety we had forgotten a bag at the Consulate and had to return to get it. Despite this entire series of events, we managed to arrive at the airport nearly on time.

It was still uncertain, however, whether they would allow me to travel with just the certification from the Consulate. They had forewarned me at the Consulate that I also needed certification of loss of passport from police headquarters, which was not feasible to obtain that day. Nevertheless, the miracle happened, and I passed the check-in without any difficulties. Everything went very well with the grace and help of Saint Nikiforos. I thank him greatly, for a second time, from the bottom of my heart.

A.K.
Theologian, Elatochori, Pieria

A spiritual child of Elder Evmenios related:
"Elder Evmenios always answered my questions patiently, including personal questions relating to his illness and his friends and relatives. Once I asked him if he, too, had a spiritual father. He told me that he was a spiritual child of Elder Nikiforos. It was the first time I had heard that name. 'Where is he?' I asked. 'I have him here.' he answered. 'He's in the cell next door.' He reverently opened the door for me to understand—to my great surprise—what he meant when he said, 'I have him here.'"

Elder Nikiforos had reposed in 1964 and Father Evmenios kept his holy relics in a poor, humble chest as a priceless treasure.

A 28-year-old who had much reverence for Saint Nikiforos, had in his possession a very small piece of his holy relics. He would often read the Supplicatory Canon to the saint, seeking help with his serious health problems and overall support in his life.

Many times when he was facing a serious problem, he would sense a fragrance coming from the saint's relics, which he always kept with him. This grace from the saint would fill him with strength and consolation.

One day when he was walking down the road, he saw ahead of him a kiosk full of various magazines. He prayed within himself, saying, "My saint, please help me to pass by this kiosk without seeing anything that might disturb or scandalize me." After he safely passed the kiosk and proceeded a little further, the saint's relics began exuding fragrance. The young man was filled with joy that the saint had immediately heard his prayer.

May 9, 2008

My name is E.N. and I feel obligated to share a few words about the miracles Saint Nikiforos the Leper has worked for me.

I learned about Saint Nikiforos from a close friend of mine at a very difficult time in my life. I was under a great deal of stress and very anxious. I was writing my graduate thesis. The topic my professor had assigned was particularly difficult for me. When I read Saint Nikiforos' book, I was especially moved. Indeed, I began calling upon him for help.

Time was passing and there was no end in sight to my thesis. I needed even more time to finish, but was ashamed to approach my professor again. I had already put myself in a bad position by repeatedly asking for extensions and lacked the courage to ask for another.

I begged Saint Nikiforos to help me. Sure enough, one time when I was crying piteously and asking for his assistance, as I was holding his book and gazing at his icon, it seemed to me that his clothing became lifelike.

The next morning my professor called. For some reason, he told me that I could take another four-day extension and not to rush. My joy was indescribable. As time passed, however, I began to have different thoughts, that perhaps it had nothing to do with the saint but was merely a coincidence....

During that time, my friend who had loaned me the book kept telling me to write a few words about the intervention of the saint. I just did not think it was really necessary and was trying to avoid it. I justified myself with the thought that, if it were merely a coincidence, I would be misleading people by writing about it.

Meanwhile, months passed until one day (at that time I was encountering other serious problems) my same friend urged me to call on Saint Nikiforos again, and also to write a few words about his assistance with my thesis. Although I told her that I would write, at the same time I was beset by different thoughts and almost began to doubt his holiness.

That same day when I returned home, I began to feel a tremendous pain that I had never before experienced. I thought something was seriously wrong with me and was very frightened....

Then I remembered how my friend had told me to call on Saint Nikiforos. I immediately recalled what I had just been thinking about the saint. I was ashamed and repented deeply for having entertained the slightest doubt about his holiness. I immediately felt the need to seek his forgiveness. I begged him to intercede for me to get well and promised myself that as soon as I felt better I would write about him.

Before I managed to finish the words of my prayer, the pain subsided. I can say with all certainty that the pain lasted for the exact amount of time necessary for me to realize how wrongly I had been thinking and to repent.

One night in my sleep I saw a monk—just simply like that. He did not speak to me or do anything else. I did not give a second thought as to the significance of my dream.

However, the next day I went to visit the monastery of Stavrovouni. When I went to the monastery's bookstore I came across the book of Saint Nikiforos on the desk of the monk managing the bookstore. As soon as I saw the icon on the cover, I realized that the monk I had seen in my sleep was Saint Nikiforos. I purchased the book and finished reading it within half an hour. The monk in the bookstore told me that the saint's relics are continually fragrant.

G.G.

Cyprus

I am being so bold as to write to you concerning your book that so elegantly and expressively sets forth the life of our ascetic father, Nikiforos Tzanakakis.

This book is a spiritual treasure, a beacon shedding light and bringing warmth in a time of spiritual coldness, when values and relations are being redefined in such a way that debases and reduces them to lower levels.

In his biography, our ascetic father Nikiforos is presented to the common reader in a truly special manner, demonstrating as faithfully as possible his high spiritual stature and revealing him to the conscience of the faithful as an example of patience, a model of unceasing prayer, and a firm support of asceticism and monasticism. Through these spiritual achievements, he has become a chosen vessel of the Holy Spirit and a speedy helper for faithful Christians who call upon him reverently in times of need.

His exceptionally sweet and peaceful appearance is overpowering, and his gaze, penetrating like a spiritual x-ray, grants people a divine consolation and strength in the difficulties and problems they face.

Certainly, all the saints who adorn the Church Triumphant are protectors and intercessors to the Lord for the faithful who honor their spiritual contests and achievements. But each star differs from another in brightness, glory, and magnitude. Likewise, this new spiritual star of our Church, Saint Nikiforos the Leper, will be distinguished from this time forth for the consolation and spiritual refuge he provides for all people who call upon his help.

His intervention is immediate and effective, as is testified by the irrefutable witness of the faithful who take refuge in his grace.

I personally have two instances to relate:

1) My wife and I, in our attempt to have a child, scheduled a relatively minor gynecological procedure at a clinic in Thessaloniki one afternoon. The procedure, although simple, presented some degree of difficulty because my wife was susceptible to allergic reactions and would have a difficult time with the anesthesia. I might also add that, inadvertently, she had not properly prepared herself. She had eaten a light meal just an hour before the procedure, because, due to her strenuous and toilsome occupation, her blood pressure had dropped and she was not feeling well. The procedure needed to take place on the second or third day of her monthly cycle, and if it were postponed it would have to wait until the next month. The gynecologist and the anesthesiologist decided to overlook the incident and continue with the procedure. But, of course, my wife had also downplayed the quantity of food she consumed, not wanting to postpone the procedure.

When the doctors took her in for the operation, I waited in the lobby together with my wife's mother. I was tightly holding the Holy Service book of Saint Nikiforos in my hands and reading along. When I had finished, I began to read his synaxarion to my mother-in-law because she was persistently asking me to tell her about this saint whose icon she did not recognize.

Shortly before I finished reading, I heard the doctor's voice from inside and became anxious, being under the mistaken impression that something had gone wrong.

On the contrary, when I approached I discovered that everything went well, that the procedure had positive results and no complications. I firmly believe that Saint Nikiforos helped us, as we were entreating him with exceptional fervor.

2) For a long time—from the moment I first read his book in 2006—I fervently begged Saint Nikiforos to come close to me with his physical presence also, by blessing me with the grace of his holy relics.

My petition was heard and I soon acquired a portion of the ascetic father's holy relics, granted to me by an Athonite monk.

From the moment I took the relics into my hands to venerate them, I was impressed by the warmth they exuded and the ineffable fragrance they emitted. At times it was very strong, and at other times it disappeared completely.

The grace of the holy relics of Saint Nikiforos is indeed great. I feel as if I have him beside me, and whenever I ask him to help me with any problem, he immediately provides a solution. He is my companion and comforter in the difficult ascent of my life's journey.

A.P.
Thessaloniki

My name is J.M. and I would like to express my gratitude and wonder for a real life miracle of Saint Nikiforos that I experienced.

It was Monday, July 7, 2008, the day the Church remembers Saint Kyriake, and I attended the Divine Liturgy in her honor. In the church there was an icon of Saint Nikiforos with his relics. It so happened that, at that time, under my right arm I had a large mole that had become irritated, swollen, and painful. I had in mind to visit a dermatologist because I had heard that moles should not be aggravated. But then another thought came to my mind. I called upon Saint Nikiforos and made the sign of the Cross over the mole with a small icon of him. I had been given the icon earlier that morning, along with the book of his life.

I repeated the same action two more times with faith. On the third day the mole began to shrink, and within five days it had disappeared completely.

Glorified is the name of our Holy God, through the intercessions of Saint Nikiforos.

J.M.
Eleusis

I would like to narrate something that happened to my family. Last summer, my son, Anastasios, had a serious accident. As he was diving in the ocean, he hit his head, broke his neck, and became completely paralyzed. We brought him to the hospital but the doctors were unable to help him. They performed an operation, but it was unsuccessful. This distressing news immediately began to circulate amongst my relatives, friends, and clients.

I visited the hospital every day. One day, one of my clients, Mrs. Maria, called me and said, "I want to visit Anastasios and bring him the holy relics of Saint Nikiforos the Leper." I awaited her visit with great joy because I held her in high esteem.

When she came to Anastasios' room, she greeted him and talked with him about his accident. After a few minutes, I told him that she had brought holy relics for him to venerate, and that he should ask Saint Nikiforos to make him well quickly.

When we brought the relics towards my son's head for him to venerate, he sensed a very beautiful fragrance. My sister-in-law, who was sitting next to me, was very perplexed. She asked if I smelled anything but I told her that I did not.

After Anastasios venerated the relics, the rest of us also venerated in turn. Mrs. Maria said that she would leave the holy relics with us for three days. We put them beside Tasos' pillow (Tasos is a nickname for Anastasios) and left the room because he was exhausted and wanted to sleep. I returned to the room from time to time to see how he was doing.

At some point, while I was sitting by my son's side as he slept, he opened his eyes and asked me, "Dad, who is the Pappouli rubbing my legs?" I did not know what he was talking about. "There's no one here," I told him. "Go back to sleep." He said to me again, "But he's right there! Don't you see him?" and he pointed to his feet. Then he said, "Oh, the

Pappouli left now." Hearing these words sent chills down my spine. This happened in the summer, in the beginning of July 2009.

My sister also attests that every time she read Saint Nikiforos' Supplicatory Canon for the restoration of our Tasos' health, she sensed an ineffable fragrance coming from his relics.

Our little Tasos became well with the help of Saint Nikiforos, and is now in Germany undergoing physical therapy. I will always be grateful to Saint Nikiforos and glorify him with all my heart for showing such great kindness towards my child.

A.T.

A lady from the island of Crete related the following miraculous interventions of the saint in the life of her family.

1) My husband, Stavros, was working in the office of our son, George. Around 10 p.m., the drill broke and he was not able to continue working. This was problematic because the job needed to be finished by the next day. I prayed and asked Saint Nikiforos for help, and the damage to the drill was rectified immediately.

2) One day, I was being bombarded constantly with critical thoughts about a certain person. The situation was tormenting me. Finally I could not stand it and called on

Saint Nikiforos, asking for his assistance. Not only was I freed from the thoughts but my whole disposition towards that person changed.

3) My son, George, is a mechanical engineer and submits engineering calculations for approval from City Planning. On one occasion, the planning office of a certain city was giving him a difficult time with some calculations he had submitted. The day that he was going to the office for his fourth attempt to have them approved, he called me on the phone and said, "Mom, I'm going to City Planning. Say a prayer for me."

Indeed I prayed, calling on Saint Nikiforos, and the calculations were approved without even being examined again.

4) George works at a manufacturing company. He was once assigned a job that would take just a few days. However, he was hoping to receive an offer to continue working with that specific company, as had some of his co-workers.

I noticed that he was troubled and uneasy. I prayed to Saint Nikiforos seeking help, and—what a miracle!—that same day he got exactly the offer he was looking for.

I give thanks to Saint Nikiforos. My heart is truly grateful to him for the assistance he provides to me and to my family.

I am 22 years old and a senior undergraduate at the Athonite Ecclesiastical Academy of the Holy Mountain. I would like, with the fear of God, to relate a miraculous incident I recently experienced with the most venerable Elder Nikiforos.

One evening, I went to say my prayers in the school's chapel. While I was venerating the icons I noticed a monk, off to the side, praying with a very large prayer rope. I made the sign of the Cross, approached him, bowed before him, and said, "Your blessing, Father." "May the Lord bless you, my child," he replied. Then he raised his head, and with a peaceful smile looked straight into my eyes. I cannot describe what strange feelings I had at that moment. I began to ask the elder some questions: "Elder, what is your name?" "My name is Nikiforos, my child, and I am from the Holy Unmercenaries," he replied.

Then he began to tell me the answers to certain questions that were troubling me at the time. He even knew my thoughts. I was astonished at the things he was telling me. Furthermore, he advised me to always say the prayer, "Lord Jesus Christ, have mercy on me the sinner." He told me to be obedient to my spiritual father, and to exercise humility and patience.

I asked him if he would give me his blessing to come and visit him some time, and he told me, "Yes, my child, come. I will await your visit with great joy. Know that I will always be praying for you."

After he blessed me, he said to me, "May Panagia be with you. And don't be afraid, my child. Have faith and patience in your trials and temptations, and I will be beside you." I bowed before him and thanked him with tears in my eyes. He embraced me and said, "Don't cry—I will always be beside you." I left the church assuming that this monk must be an acquaintance of our dean. Half an hour later, something urged me to go back inside the church. When I entered, all I found was a very intense fragrance. I did not say anything to anyone.

A few days later, a certain monk gave me a book. As soon as I saw the photograph and the name on the cover, I burst into tears. The icon portrayed the Elder Nikiforos.

I thank God that he counted me worthy to meet the saint. From the time of our encounter in the chapel, I feel a special love for him and hold him in great reverence. I often have the vivid sensation that he is beside me.

L.G.
Seminarian

In June of 2009, our baby was born prematurely in the Papageorgiou Hospital of Thessaloniki.

That same month, because of the baby's health, we were transported by helicopter to Saint Sophia Children's Hospital in Athens. During our stay there, which lasted about two months, we became acquainted with Saint Nikiforos the Leper through a book that had been given to us by an Athonite elder.

Our newborn baby had respiratory and cardiac problems. The doctors told us that he was not doing very well and would eventually need surgical intervention. This is why he was not eating normally and since he was not able to eat from a bottle, we could not take him home. He was still being fed with a tube. Every day our anxiety increased and we did not know what to think about the situation. The baby was in intensive care, and during the two half-hour visiting periods permitted to us every day, we saw that sometimes he was better and other times worse.

Seeing all that was happening and sharing in our pain, the Athonite elder who gave us the book entrusted to us the holy relics of Saint Nikiforos the Leper inside a small reliquary box. He told us, "For three days, when you go to see your baby, make the sign of the Cross with the holy relics over the incubator." And so in the morning, after we read the Supplicatory Canon to the saint, we went to the ICU and blessed our baby, along with all the other babies. In the afternoon, while we were waiting for our second visit together with the other parents, the on-call doctor who was monitoring the newborns that day came out and said, "I don't know what happened but all the babies are well today. I have nothing more to say; I can't explain it."

We looked at each other in amazement and smiled. Saint Nikiforos was quick to hear our prayers and show his love.

The next few mornings we visited our baby and continued to pray over him and bless him with the relics.

The doctors were telling us that it would take a very long time for him to be able to start drinking from a bottle. But within just a few days, when we arrived for our morning visit, we were struck with amazement. Our little boy was drinking from a bottle and eating very well. "You will be able to take him home in four or five days," the doctor told us in wonder.

Indeed, five days later we brought our baby home. We are very thankful to Saint Nikiforos for the love he showed us.

A. and D.S.

My first encounter with Saint Nikiforos was on January 4, 2009, the day of his commemoration. I was in Athens, soon to be admitted to the hospital, having been diagnosed with a 7.5 cm tumor and other smaller tumors in my liver.

That day I received a phone call from Corfu, from the hieromonk Father Polycarp who told me briefly about Saint Nikiforos and encouraged me to go and venerate his relics. Indeed, I went immediately and felt an instant attraction to the saint. I venerated his holy relics, talked for a little while with the saint, and then left.

The day of the surgery was approaching, when they were to remove almost three quarters of my liver. It was going to be a difficult operation, but during the days prior, Saint Nikiforos was continually in my mind. I felt him next to me continually.

The day before the surgery I went to visit the saint again and entreated him with all my heart to help me. This time, his relics were fragrant. I would even go so far as to say that the intensity of the fragrance was intoxicating. My wife was also there with me. The saint made such an impression on her as well that from that time she promised the saint that she would be the godmother for a baby boy and give him the name Nikiforos at his baptism.

All this time, I had been drawing strength from Saint Nikiforos. I went into surgery with a calm composure and without fear. Likewise, my post-surgical recovery time passed without difficulties or anxiety.

As the attending doctors had informed my family, my condition was very grave and they had determined that I only had a few months to live. I learned this a year later, after I had become completely well.

I thank Saint Nikiforos for the help he provided me at the most difficult and critical moment in my life.

J.L.
Corfu

January 27, 2010

A lady from Sydney, Australia, related the following: A monk from the Holy Mountain, Father Palladios, had given her a book about Saint Nikiforos as a gift on one of his visits. "When I opened the book to read it, it exuded a sweet fragrance," she continued. "I was deeply moved and read it with great respect. I had never experienced anything like that before, even though I have read many books about saints. When I finished reading Saint Nikiforos' book, I didn't put it together with my other books. Instead, I placed it in a special cabinet in which I also keep holy icons. I put it there to keep it as a blessing, and especially so that the fragrance would not go away."

D.
Sydney, Australia

With this letter I wish to inform you of an incident that I personally believe is a miracle of Saint Nikiforos the Leper and wonderworker (my beloved Pappouli).

One of my mother's aunts, Eleni, was not feeling well. She was admitted to the Hippocratic Hospital of Thessaloniki for examinations on January 11, 2010. The doctors determined that liquid was collecting in her lungs. Her children were very concerned and the news spread like wildfire among all our relatives. When I heard the news from my mother, I included her name with those I commemorated when I read the Supplicatory Canon to the saint that afternoon. I was sure that he would do something to help.

Truly the miracle happened. The saint granted his assistance immediately and by the next morning her health had greatly improved. Indeed, when one of her daughters went to visit her that morning in the hospital, she found her in a very good condition. She immediately called my mother, saying, "What did you do that made my mother well? It's as if she has been resurrected!" Of course she was released from the hospital shortly after and has been home ever since.

J.L.
Student of Pastoral and Social Theology,
Aristotelian University of Thessaloniki

January 1, 2010

I have great respect and love for Saint Nikiforos. To me, he is a great saint who hastens to help and support me at every difficult moment of my life. I also see his miraculous presence in the lives of others, as they themselves confess.

One of my business' better customers faced a serious problem in his own enterprise, and had given up all hope of resolving it.

On New Year's Day, I took the small piece of Saint Nikiforos' holy relics that I have in my possession and brought it to my shop so that my work would be blessed that year. As I was leaving, I decided to pass by my customer's business also, asking the saint to help resolve his tremendously difficult situation that had been dragging on for so long. Within a few days, I learned that this long-standing problem had been completely resolved. I thanked the saint from the depths of my soul that he heard my humble prayer and responded immediately.

C. G.
Herakleion, Crete

The event that bonded us deeply with Saint Nikiforos occurred in August 2009, during a period of time that was very difficult for me and my wife. Our second child was in the ICU for newborns in critical condition, and our anxiety and worry was doubly intense, as we had just lost our first child the previous year.

That day, my wife began to read Saint Nikiforos' book, which we had recently acquired. As she was reading, an ineffable fragrance suddenly exuded from the book. She immediately exclaimed to me that the book was fragrant and asked me if I smelled the same thing that she smelled. I was sitting next to her, and as I moved a little closer to where she was holding the book, I immediately confirmed that I, too, sensed the fragrance. But what was even more special about that moment was the spiritual uplifting that accompanied the fragrance—a consolation and spiritual sweetness that created a bond between the saint and us. Until that moment Saint Nikiforos was unknown to us. He came into our hearts with this gift of consolation and he remains there in our heart to this day. Because of this incident, we became more interested in the saint, sought to learn more about his life and conceived the desire to venerate his holy relics.

Indeed, ever since then, when we hear his name we are filled with reverence and seek his help in every difficult situation of our life. I also began to feel an unprecedented urge to distribute books with the life of the saint to my friends and acquaintances.

M.M.
Physical Therapist

December 15, 2011

Reverend Father Simon,
    I am a resident of the island of Mytilene. I am writing to tell you about my acquaintance with Saint Nikiforos the Leper, how I came to visit you and venerate his holy relics, and the many miraculous signs he has worked for me.

About three years ago, I first heard of the existence of the saint from an internet friend of mine on Facebook.

Two summers ago (2010) I took a vacation to Germany. On Sunday I attended the Divine Liturgy at a Greek Orthodox Church, together with an acquaintance.

After the dismissal, the parish council was selling various items and I decided to buy something to support them. There, remarkably, they had a book about Saint

Nikiforos the Leper, written by a certain monk Simon. I bought the book and we left. To be honest, I was exceptionally pleased to find the book because I had not found much on the internet concerning the life of the saint.

I started reading the book and was truly amazed by how much the saint suffered from a young age. It gave me hope for all the suffering that afflicts the world. I began to wonder how I could find a church or a monastery where I could venerate the relics of the saint. There was nothing mentioned in the book; I found nothing online—nothing in Crete, nothing in Chios, nothing anywhere. Time was passing. Meanwhile, I don't know why, but I had placed the book on the desk in my bedroom instead of filing it away on the bookshelf.

September came and I commenced some very difficult post-graduate work, with a heavy workload and frequent attendance at the university. I worked from 9 a.m. to 4 or 5 p.m., and then attended classes until 9 p.m.—a full 12-hour day, and then I needed to study. Where was I going to find endurance? Where would I find strength? Nonetheless, whenever I became tired I would pick up the saint's book, say an urgent prayer and instantly regain my strength. So much so, that I received a scholarship in Austria for the following summer (2011), and was also accepted to teach as an assistant professor at the Aegean Institute for a semester. All of this was with the help of the saint. With a simple, "Help me, O saint." A simple supplication.

Time passed, and I still desired to venerate the relics of the saint.

I went to Athens for surgery.

When I was released from the hospital the day after the operation, although I was in a lot of pain, I decided not to return directly to Mytilene but to go and venerate my saint.

My desire was fulfilled in a wondrous way. I received a small piece of the saint's relics from a monk there, as well as other blessings. I immediately ordered a wood-carved reliquary box to protect them.

After my operation, I suffered an infection. The opening from my incision was not healing and was letting out pus with an unpleasant stench, along with blood and other impurities. I went to the hospital and they cleaned it for me, but it was painful and kept excreting liquid. I called my doctor who prescribed a treatment for me, but it didn't help and he asked me to return to Athens for him to examine it. I remembered the boldness of the saint and asked him to work his miracle. "Come on, my saint," I told him, "do something. Come on, my saint, do something." And I'm not exaggerating: all the running fluid stopped immediately. I went to the doctor and he told me, "You came for no reason. There's nothing wrong with you."

With awe and reverence,

E.P.
Educator

During a period of time in my life when I was struggling with great disappointment from a broken relationship, I began to make frequent visits to monasteries and elders. I was trying to make myself feel better, but also to find myself. One of the monasteries I visited was dedicated to Saint Paraskeve in Mazion of Megara. There I encountered a very sympathetic monk who gave me a little icon of Saint Nikiforos. It contained a small piece of his holy relics. He told me to keep the saint with me at all times, without exception. From that time on, I felt like Saint Nikiforos was always with me—beside me, near me, next to me at my every step. It was he who truly helped me get back on my feet and overcome my challenges.

I received so much grace from the saint that I ended up loving the saint incomparably more than the woman I had been in a relationship with. The saint became my symbol of victory, as his name "Nikiforos" translates.

Around the same time, I had a meeting with a very significant person. I prayed to the saint for all to go well with this encounter. And truly, everything went very well. After the meeting, I felt that I had truly managed to emerge victorious again.

Furthermore, the saint helped me to find a job, to become more sociable, and—most importantly—to befriend spiritual people who are close to God.

I extend my heartfelt thanks to the saint who helped me and continues to help me.

P.C., 25 years old

Piraeus, 2010

Father Evlogios, a hieromonk of the Holy Monastery of Saint Paraskeve in Mazion of Megara, narrated a miracle that Saint Nikiforos worked for one of his cousins.

Demetrios, a 17-year-old, had a serious health issue that was causing intense pains in the area of his reproductive organs, but was ashamed to say anything about it. With time, however, his condition became worse. When he could not endure any longer he finally informed his family. They took him to Saint Savvas' hospital on the day of Theophany, 2011. After many examinations the doctors determined that he had cancer. It had spread to such an extent that they were not able to do anything. They gave the boy a few weeks, if not just days, to live.

Father Evlogios' mother, young Demetrios' aunt, had much reverence for Saint Nikiforos and began to read his biography as a sort of supplication to the saint for the boy to become well. As soon as she would finish reading it, she started over again, all the while fervently entreating the saint to make her nephew well.

Little by little, the young man's condition began to improve. His pains decreased and when they brought him back to the hospital shortly before Pascha, the doctors determined that the boy was completely cured. They repeated the examinations and found no signs of cancer.

Everyone was jumping for joy at the news. The boy's aunt could not find words to thank Saint Nikiforos. She kept shouting, "This is a miracle of Saint Nikiforos! This is a miracle of Saint Nikiforos!"

Later, she requested from her son, the hieromonk, an icon of the saint to have him as her own guardian as well.

I n July of 2009, I visited a monk (who has now reposed) at his cell on the Holy Mountain. When I came inside, he went to bring me some water and as he entered the kitchen I heard him saying to someone, "Nikiforos, we'll talk later. I have company right now." I was taken aback and when the monk returned I asked him, "Who is Nikiforos, Pappouli?" "He is a worthy struggler of patience and prayer," he told me. "Do I know him?" I asked. "You will learn about him," he replied. "What do you mean by that?" I inquired. Then he related to me the following incident:

"I recently learned of a woman who was diagnosed with cancer. She was married and would leave behind five children, the oldest being only 9 years old. So I decided to pray to God to give me the cancer because I'm an old man and I don't need to live any longer. While I was saying this prayer—daydreamer that I am—I saw an enormous cloud carrying twelve elders, one of whom I did not recognize. I asked for their blessing, and the unknown elder said that our Lord sent them to tell me that nobody can take upon his own shoulders the cross that God has given someone else to bear, because that would be stealing the other person's crown. Likewise, the unknown elder told me that I already carry much and should not seek more. After all this, I asked the unknown elder on the cloud what his name was and he told me, 'Nikiforos the Leper, and because of your love and self-denial, I will heal the woman.'"

When the monk finished his account, I asked him, "And did the woman become well?" "Yes, she did," he told me. Then he added, with a little laugh, "but I still ask the Lord why He didn't give me the cancer."

Although he told me not to speak of this incident, I am revealing it to you since I consider it to be a remarkable testimony concerning Saint Nikiforos.

Father Theologos Gasparatos

T he first time I read the book, *Saint Nikiforos the Leper,* in its 1st edition years ago, I was impressed by the saint's endurance and perseverance in the adversities of his life.

It was with pain in my heart that I read how he was brought from Chios to the Holy Unmercenaries at the Hospital for Infectious Diseases in Athens. I am familiar with this illness from my studies, so I had an even greater admiration for the great strength and courage he had found through the Faith.

During the time period that I was reading the book, I was suffering from allergy-related nasal polyps that should have been removed a long time before. I could only breathe from my mouth, not from my nose at all, and had completely lost my sense of smell.

I had accepted and become accustomed to my loss of smell, but suddenly, while I was reading the part of the saint's book that talked about his transfer to the Hospital for Infectious Diseases, I began to sense an aroma of basil or rose or jasmine. I could not determine exactly what it was, but it was very striking.

I set the book down and went out to the balcony to find the fragrant flower, but saw nothing. Then I went to the kitchen and tried smelling various items, such as fruit, to see if they were fragrant.

None of these things, however, smelled like the first aroma. And it was at that moment that I realized what was happening: I could smell again. Moreover, just to be sure that I had truly regained my sense of smell, I opened a little jar of coffee, and sure enough, I could smell it. That was it! I exclaimed: "My God, this is a miracle! It is the blessing of my acquaintance with Saint Nikiforos and my deep love and respect for him." The memory of this blessed moment has accompanied me through all my life's difficulties. And his miracles are not limited to only this...

My friends who know the saint have also experienced miracles of his grace. I have a small icon with a little piece of the relics of Saint Nikiforos, and I allow my friends to borrow it so that they too might receive benefit. One friend had failed her driver's test many times. When she had this icon of the saint with her, she was finally able to overcome her fear and anxiety, and came across as an experienced driver. The saint had even provided for there to be a new driving instructor that day. From that time on, she has Saint Nikiforos as the guardian of her car.

Another friend, a working woman, went back to night school in order to fulfill her dream of becoming a teacher. Because she had limited time and no tutor, she was not able to master all the material for her history course. I offered her the icon of Saint Nikiforos to help her with her exams and she agreed to take it. It happened that the topic appearing on the exam was the only one she knew very well and she passed with a grade of 19.5 (on a scale of 20). Great is the grace of Saint Nikiforos. My friend continued to call on the saint throughout her years as a student of Education.

H.T.
Herakleion, Crete

November 11, 2011

Father Simon,
I was given the book, *Nikiforos the Leper, the Glorious Athlete of Endurance,* by a pious lady, but had not read it. However, I had learned of some of the saint's miracles from the radio station of the Church of Piraeus.

Recently, I was experiencing intense pains in my back and groin. On November 10, 2011, I heard of the miracle of the 14-year-old boy who was paralyzed after diving in the ocean but began to walk with the help of Saint Nikiforos. Spontaneously, I asked the saint to help me also, God's unworthy servant, by relieving me of my pains and healing the illness that was affecting my body. Glory be to God! I immediately sensed that my condition changed and I was healed through the intercessions of Saint Nikiforos the Leper. (I have not even examined what the exact cause of the pain might have been, believing simply that "all things are possible" for our Holy Triune God).

Wondrous is God in His saints!

V.V.
Athens

Your blessing, Father Simon! The following incident occurred yesterday, on October 19. When I brought my three children home from school, I decided to put all our bags in the elevator because they were heavy and I was carrying the baby. We ascended the stairs of our apartment building on foot. When I pressed the button to bring the elevator up from ground level to the first floor, nothing happened. I went back downstairs and tried to open the elevator door, but it would not open. I tried again—nothing. I went upstairs again and pushed the button, but again, nothing.

I rang the bell to get help from the manager. He was not there, but I spoke with his wife who told me that the elevator company had already come in the morning to fix it. She called them again but they said they would not be able to come back that day—perhaps in the afternoon, but more likely, the next morning. I asked for the company's phone number and went inside my apartment (fortunately I had at least my house key and cell phone on me). I called my husband and told him to call the company and ask them to come today because my purse (which contained a significant amount of money, ID cards, my passport, residence permit, etc.) and our three children's school bags were all stuck inside the elevator.

I began to panic. My oldest son was worried that he would not be able to do his homework or bring his books to school the following day. I was afraid that if the elevator door finally opened and I was not there, someone might come and steal my purse. It was then that I thought to pray to Elder Nikiforos. I picked up his book and told him, "Help us, Elder Nikiforos, I beg you. I don't know what is going to happen." I also said, "I believe. Lord, help my unbelief." I made the sign of the Cross and kissed the icon on the cover of the book. A minute later I heard my neighbor opening her door, and went to tell her what had happened so that she would be aware of the situation. My neighbor went to the elevator door, and it opened immediately.

I almost wept from joy and wonder. When I returned to my apartment I went to thank the Elder, again kissing his icon and making the sign of the Cross.

That evening, I sang some of the hymns in honor of the saint. I have not told anyone else, not even my husband, about this miracle.

C.M.

Athens – June 7, 2010

To the most venerable monk Simon:

With the present letter I would like to relate to you the miracle that happened to me through the divine intervention of our holy and God-bearing father, Nikiforos the Leper.

From a young age I have struggled with serious diabetes. As a result, from time to time I have liver problems that aggravate my health in general. At the suggestion of my doctor I was scheduled for a liver examination at the Annunciation Hospital on May 4, 2010. She believed that my condition was especially dangerous and that part of my liver had already been irreparably damaged.

This made me very pensive and I remained enclosed in my cell for many days, praying with tears. On May 11th, I would learn the results of the examinations. I prayed even more fervently on the day before. As I was praying, I had the thought to call upon Saint Nikiforos the Leper whom I had learned of a few years ago while visiting the Holy Mountain. Thus, I spent the whole night in vigil, calling upon the help of the Panagia and of Saint Nikiforos.

The next morning, while my anxiety was at its peak as I waited to learn how much of my liver had been damaged, I was amazed to hear the doctor announce to me the pleasant news that there was no need to worry because my examination was clear.

In order to confirm the results I repeated the examination that same day, and on May 18th I received the results showing that my liver was healthy. The doctors were bewildered.

I am convinced that this miracle of God's providence is due to the persuasive intercessions of Saint Nikiforos whom I now look upon as my unsleeping guardian and protector. I am going to order an icon of him to have in my cell.

With love in Christ,

Monk Asterios Apostolou

Holy Monastery of the Bodiless Powers, Petrakis

One day Father Constantine Vastakis came and served Liturgy at our little Kellion in Athens. His wife accompanied him.

While he was distributing the blessed bread at the end of the Liturgy, his presvytera inquired, "Where is the other priest?" We all replied, "What other priest? There was no other priest here." Then Presvytera said, "During the service, I saw a priest come in, venerate that icon of the Panagia standing across from us, and proceed towards the room next door." But she was left wondering who this priest might have been.

She told us the next day that when they had come for the Liturgy and venerated the holy relics of Saint Nikiforos, she had smelled an ineffable fragrance and thought, "They must have put a lot of perfume on these relics." But that night she saw the saint in her sleep. She saw his face up close, just as it is depicted in his icon, with the same koukoulion (monastic head covering), and recognized him as the "priest" she had seen during the Divine Liturgy.

A few months later, the same presvytera told us that while she was listening to a radio broadcast of Saint Nikiforos' book from the Church of Piraeus, she saw the saint standing next to her icons in the corner of the room. When the program finished, around 1:30-2:00 a.m., an intensely fragrant aroma flooded the room. She immediately began thanking the saint for honoring her with his presence and giving her joy.

An account of a monk concerning Saint Nikiforos the Leper:

An acquaintance of mine who is from the city of Larissa had read the life of Saint Nikiforos. When she became pregnant, the doctors told her that she would have a girl.

One night she saw Saint Nikiforos in a dream telling her that when she gives birth she should name her child Nikiforos. She was surprised and told the saint that the doctors said she would have a girl, not a boy. Saint Nikiforos assured her that the child is a boy and that she should name him Nikiforos. The woman awoke in wonder and amazement at what she had dreamed and was unable

to explain it. When she went for her next prenatal examination, the doctor told her that they were mistaken the
first time, and that the child is a boy—and this indeed
was confirmed when the child was born.

Hieromonk Luke

Holy Monastery of Xenophon

Mount Athos

January 8, 2012

Our reverend Father Simon,
We would like to add our own story to your collection of the miracles of Saint Nikiforos.

Our iconographer, Sister Evsevia, broke her right
arm just after we had received an order to paint the icons
for the iconostasis of the church of Saint Parthenios of
Lampsacus.

One evening during the time she was in a cast,
she heard the life and miracles of Saint Nikiforos from
the radio station of the Church of Piraeus. She was very
touched by his life and fervently begged the saint to heal
her, promising that she would paint his icon. That same
moment, she was suddenly able to move her stiffened
fingers without feeling any pain.

When her cast was removed, her hand was completely restored to its former function after just two sessions of physical therapy, and she began to paint icons for
the iconostasis. As soon as she finishes, she will begin the
saint's icon as she promised.

With boldness, we ask you if it is possible to send a small piece of his relics to our monastery to help us in our spiritual struggle.

With gratitude and respect,

Nun Agnes
Abbess of the Holy Monastery of
Panagia Eleousa, Kalymnos

January 2012

A certain nun suffered with severe vertigo and chronic pains for more than 20 years. She could not stand straight, nor turn left or right, and as time passed her condition had become worse.

Five months ago she came across the book with Saint Nikiforos' biography. The nun was touched by his life and began to beg him fervently: "My saint, you endured so much pain and suffered so much during your life. Take away my vertigo and heal my head—I cannot bear it any more."

She became well immediately and never had to take medications again.

From a telephone communication

Towards the beginning of October 2011, I received a visit from a court official announcing that my

business would be auctioned on November 30, 2011, because I had signed as guarantor for my husband's debt.

I was deeply troubled and concerned. I did not know what to do because all of my savings had gone to my husband's serious matters. After I received this news, I could only sleep for 2 or 3 hours each night. The rest of the time I was awake, trying in the midst of my terrible anxiety to find a way to stop the auction. The total debt was 26,000 euros and the bank was demanding that 20,000 be paid immediately. The days were passing, the auction was approaching, but the only money I came up with—leaving everything else unpaid—was 2,500 euros.

On November 10th I awoke at 6 in the morning, distraught once again. Before I could even lift the blanket off my head, I was already thinking, "What am I going to do about the debt?" I did not have time to finish my thought, when suddenly, on my right, the figure of a standing monk appeared out of nowhere. I threw the covers off and sat up straight in bed, saying, "Oh my God! What was that?" and made the sign of the Cross. I looked around and saw nothing. I turned on the radio in order to hear something, anything at all, to calm my nerves at that hour.

What happened then was incredible, a true miracle. The radio was tuned to the station of the Church of Piraeus, which at that moment was broadcasting the life of Saint Nikiforos the Leper. It was about halfway through the program. I listened attentively and, forgetting about my own problem, I became absorbed in the torments of Saint

Nikiforos, grieving over them and being moved to tears. I said to myself, "Don't worry, it's in God's hands."

I began to search for the saint's biography in various bookstores. After three attempts I still had not found it, so I placed an order for it. When I finally received the book, I was shocked and remained speechless: the icon on the cover of the book depicted the same figure that had come and stood beside me that night. How was it that at that moment I went to turn on the radio, when I had passed so many other sleepless nights and never thought to do such a thing? I took the book and read it, and then read it again. I prayed to Saint Nikiforos and on the 30th of November I set out for the auction with my 2,500 euros, calm and joyful, without any anxiety. I had regained my peace and composure, and I had not been waking up with nightmares any more.

Up until 11 o' clock in the morning on November 30, 2011, the bank was still demanding 20,000 euros. I continued to pray to Saint Nikiforos to help me. I was dealing with people who were not showing any understanding at all and I was going to lose my business. At 11:30, something happened that I will never forget as long as I live. My cell phone rang. Once again, it was the harsh banker who had been demanding the 20,000 euros. But this time his voice was completely different—it was calm, almost divine—and he told me, "Do you have 2,000-2,500 euros to give us so we can stop the auction?"

I fell to my knees and could not stop weeping. Saint Nikiforos was continually beside me, from that dawn when

I first encountered him until that moment when I knelt down and wept. The auction was called off; they took my 2,500 euros and an arrangement was made for the debt to be paid off in installments each month. A vision, a radio program, a book—a vivid, living Saint Nikiforos who entered my life. I pray to him and thank him for helping me.

I had never, ever, heard or read anything about Saint Nikiforos the Leper. I did not even know that he existed. The saint, however, who loves and prays for all of us, heard and felt my pain and agony, and came and found me.

Thank you, my Lord Jesus Christ.

Thank you, Saint Nikiforos the Leper.

P.N.
Athens

March 4, 2012

Father Simon,

I send my regards and humbly ask for your blessing.

I learned of Saint Nikiforos from a radio broadcast of the Church of Piraeus one Saturday evening. I was touched by his life, humility and faith.

For the last few years I had been afflicted with a gynecological problem (severe hemorrhaging), and the doctors had told me that I would need to undergo a hysterectomy. As a last resort I had attempted a therapy that entailed receiving injections over a span of many months, which seemed to be working. However, if the hemorrhaging started again I would need to go for surgery without delay.

The same evening that I first heard about Saint Nikiforos, the hemorrhaging began again. I began to pray to the saint and decided to find the book about his life. I asked my cousin who works in central Athens to buy it for me as soon as she could. I waited impatiently for her to bring it to me, but instead she called me on the phone to tell me that the book had sold out and she would try to find it for me the next week. I was disappointed but kept praying to the saint every day. Meanwhile, the hemorrhaging continued. Somehow, I was not at all concerned. I believed very deeply that as soon as the book came into my hands, this condition would stop.

Fifteen days later, my cousin brought me the book. I read the whole thing in one evening and the next day I was perfectly well. From that time, I pray to Saint Nikiforos every day and ask for his help. I keep his book next to my pillow and he grants me peace and strength.

V.A.

Athens

February 22, 2012

Elder Simon,

I am writing to inform you of a miraculous event that occurred in our home in Corinth on January 29, 2012.

I learned of Saint Nikiforos the Leper from a broadcast of the Church of Piraeus one evening. I purchased his book and read it together with my wife, Maria.

We have a nephew, an eight-year-old boy, in second grade. He began to read the Life and Miracles of the saint over the three-day weekend from January 28-30th. On Sunday, around 6:00 p.m., he reached the page with the picture of the small chest that held the saint's relics. He began to shout, "Aunt Maria, there's a sweet smell coming from the book, better than incense!" He handed it to us so we could smell it too, but we did not perceive anything. My wife simply began to weep, and I exclaimed, "Wondrous is God in His saints!"

We thank Saint Nikiforos for revealing his presence to our nephew.

May all children have the saint's blessing.

With the love of Jesus Christ,

P.

Corinth

In the year 2011, I was having a financial crisis. The time was approaching for my daughter's wedding and the money I had would by no means suffice. I had serious anxiety and, unable to think of another solution, I began to play the lottery in order to solve my family's pressing problems.

One evening, I saw Saint Nikiforos in my sleep. He

introduced himself and then told me in a stern tone of voice, "Do not play the lottery ever again." It is worth noting that I had heard about the saint but did not have any special connections with him, nor did I even recognize his face. I was greatly alarmed by his austere expression. I discussed the matter with a family friend, a faithful and reliable person, who told me, "You received your message. Be more careful from now on." During this period of preparation for the wedding, the saint came to me again a second time in my sleep and told me, "I want you to come to my village." I went, solely out of obedience.

In time, our economic situation stabilized and we had a little room to breathe. The wedding also came to pass, glory be to God.

That same year, my son was facing a lawsuit at work based on an accusation concerning the former proprietor of the enterprise. Once again, more fears and anxieties. This time, however, after my previous experience with the saint, I began to read his book, *Nikiforos the Leper, Glorious Athlete of Endurance*, over and over again as a prayer. I read it so many times that I practically knew it by heart!... The court case took place and my son was exonerated.

In 2013, I attended a convention. On the first day, as I was approaching the main conference room, I smelled a wonderful aroma. At first I mistook it for some sort of perfume, but none of the ladies who were in attendance seemed to be wearing anything like it. Then I thought to myself that it must be the flowers, but when I went near them I realized that they did not have that special smell either. The rest of the day this fragrance followed me everywhere. That entire evening, even when I withdrew to my room, wherever I went, I was overpowered by that exquisite smell. On that first day I had also noticed a small icon of Saint Nikiforos that a lady had brought and placed near the speaker's podium. I did not realize that the wonderful fragrance was coming from my beloved Saint until I returned to the conference room the next day, and the air was back to normal; it had no fragrance, and the lady with the icon was not in attendance.

I hold the saint in much reverence. I consider him my dear friend, my supporter and my protector. I never go to sleep at night without "talking" to him and venerating his icon, which I keep on my nightstand. Every morning I ask him to watch over me, my family and the whole world.

Anonymous

January 13, 2013

I am writing to you from a small city in the Peloponnese, Aegium of Achaea. Last year I read your book about Saint Nikiforos the Leper. Before this, I knew nothing about him. I was very moved by his story and his way of life and immediately decided to seek his assistance with the following chronic problem of mine.

For many years I have had a number of small lipomas (fatty tumors). At first, there were about 13 of them, some of which were growing rapidly and causing pain. A few years ago I had removed three and, perhaps for that reason, the remaining tumors began multiplying dramatically. I asked the doctor who had removed the first growing tumors to remove a few more, but he recommended that I not tamper with them again at all.

I prayed fervently to the saint of God. I would make the sign of the Cross over my head with his book because it bears his icon, and within a few days I discovered, to my amazement, that the three largest tumors—which were hurting me and growing rapidly—had shrunk, and the rest of them had remained stable.

I had promised in my prayer to the saint, however, that I would write to you of his miraculous intervention, but unfortunately I neglected to do so for many months.

So it happened that one of the tumors—the only one that is visible, on my upper forehead—began to grow again because of my ingratitude. I beg you humbly, pray to the saint and intercede with him to forgive me.

I thank the saint of God very much that he heard the prayer of me, the sinner. I also thank you for the beautiful book you wrote. I wish you a holy New Year, blessed by the Lord.

With reverence, I humbly ask for your blessing,

L.P.

Aegium

January 21, 2013

I too would like to glorify once again the Holy Trinity, and Saint Nikiforos the Leper who suffered so much pain, for working his miracle for us also, the lowly servants of God.

My son was suffering from depression, an illness that tormented him and left him secluded in a dark room. He did not have the strength or desire to get out of bed, or even to eat. He hid himself under the covers and cried continually, day and night. We brought him to many doctors, but unfortunately had no positive results. We prayed continually for him to recover and not to suffer, not to be bedridden at the young age of 45.

One evening my niece came and she brought us the book of Saint Nikiforos the Leper. When she took the book out of her bag, it was fragrant! The first to venerate it was my son, who eagerly got out of bed!

The rest of us in turn also venerated the book with much faith, begging with tears for the saint to help us. After three days, during which time my son still would not get up to eat, my niece came again, this time bringing an icon of the saint that she had been given. We blessed my son, making the sign of the Cross over him with the icon, and after 20 minutes, Saint Nikiforos showed us his amazing grace.

My ailing son got out of bed, ate and began to laugh for the first time in two and a half years, as if he were a completely different person. We glorified the saint and said, "Saint Nikiforos worked a miracle!" That was the last day my son spent in bed. Since then he has returned to normal, with interest in life and work. The burning tears of pain have stopped flowing from his eyes.

I glorify the Holy Trinity that through the prayers of Saint Nikiforos my dear child has returned to work.

May the saint always be a protector and guardian both for him and for the whole world! Glorified is the holy name of Saint Nikiforos!

A.M.

Megara

February 18, 2014

My dear Father Simon, bless.

Please allow me to present my own testimony concerning Saint Nikiforos' miraculous intervention in my family.

Two years ago, my sister was diagnosed with breast cancer, albeit in an early stage. After her operation she was treated with chemotherapy and radiation at the doctors' suggestion, as a preventative measure. In October 2013, however, she had an allergic reaction to the therapies and medicine. Her whole body broke out in hives that caused terrible and painful itching. She was not able to sleep at all for two whole months and her entire body had become one giant wound from the itching. Despite the doctors' efforts, her condition became worse and worse every day. When I visited her I told her about Saint Nikiforos the Leper. Up until that moment he was completely unknown to her. I also gave her a small icon of the saint. That evening, as she told me later, she prayed to the saint and then lay down with his icon in her arms. Within a few minutes she had fallen asleep and did not wake up until the next day. When she awoke the itching was gone, and within a few days every trace of the hives had disappeared from her body.

From this experience, my family is compelled to express our gratitude to our Triune God for the great blessing He has granted to us in these latter days—this speedy, wonder-working doctor, Saint Nikiforos the Leper.

With much love in Christ,

Father Constantine Scartoulis
The Church of the Lord's Ascension, Neos Cosmos

One day before Christmas in 2011, I woke up with a severe irritation across my forehead and eye. I broke out in small pimples that caused extreme burning and itching. My whole face swelled and became disfigured. The doctor confirmed that I had shingles in that region of my face. She warned me that I would suffer much pain and gave me pills for pain management. Everyone I saw told me that I was going to suffer very much and that I might even be in pain for a whole year. It is worth mentioning that I had already been suffering from a severe disorder of the central nervous system for many years.

All this news I was being told frightened me initially.

Then I remembered Saint Nikiforos. I asked my husband to purchase the book with his Supplicatory Canon for me, and he did.

From that moment on I was no longer afraid. I knew that my good, wonder-working saint would not allow me to be in pain. And truly, the miracle happened. After that, not even for a fraction of a second did I feel pain, or even irritation. Since then, I read the Supplicatory Canon of Saint Nikiforos every day, praying and entreating him on behalf of my family and myself.

E.P.

Thessaloniki, 2011

February 20, 2012

With just a few words, I would like to tell you how my daughter and I had an argument. It was over trivial matters but we were not on speaking terms with each other for about two years. Even though she lives in the apartment above me, she would not even come down to make an appearance. In the past, however, we had a very loving relationship.

I prayed to the saint and within three or four days my door opened (my daughter always has my key with her). All of a sudden she walked in, smiling, just as I had imagined and had asked of the saint.

I thank Saint Nikiforos with all my soul.

M.A.

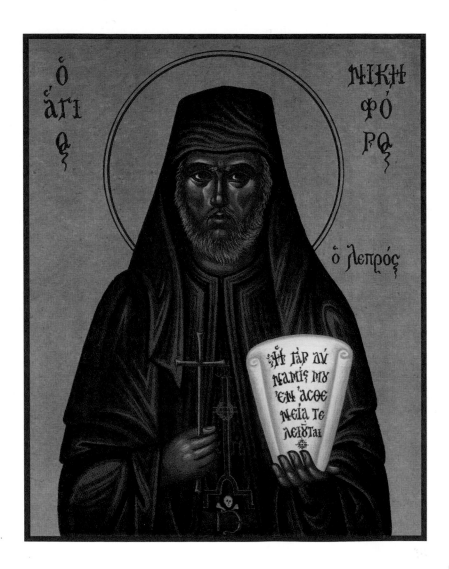

My name is K.Z. and I am 45 years old. On July 7, 2012, I was diagnosed with stage 3 cancer of the bladder. There were also high levels of metastatic cancer cells. The tumor in my bladder was 5 centimeters in size; in other words, it was half the size of my bladder.

I immediately stopped smoking, drinking alcoholic beverages and consuming sugar and gluten.

After five sessions of chemotherapy my examinations showed inflammation of the lymph nodes. The doctors told me that there was only a 10% chance of being cured. I was dying, I was terrified and I was suffering intense pain. When my family heard the news they naturally became very anxious. It was my mother who really supported me. When I first saw her praying, she was reading the service of Saint Nikiforos. I sat next to her and we prayed together to the saint. I prayed that I might be numbered among those 10% who survive the illness.

On January 29, 2013, I went in for surgery. The operation lasted eight hours. They removed my bladder and all visible cancer. The doctor, however, said that he had located further swelling of the lymph nodes, which had hardened, indicating the presence of more cancer.

I continued to pray to my saint, believing with all my heart that I was secure and that he would save me.

On March 5, 2013, it was announced to me that when the doctors had examined the lymph nodes again, there was no sign of cancer.

THE MIRACLE HAPPENED!!!

PRAYERS ARE ANSWERED!!!

I beg you all, believe!

October 28, 2012

I would like to recount to you a miracle that, by the grace of God, Saint Nikiforos accomplished for us. My husband had presented the justification necessary to collect his pension, but the tax office was demanding 5,000 euros up front before it could be released. There was no way that we could come up with that much money. I resorted to prayer, and I told our problem to an acquaintance of mine who is a Guard of the Holy Tomb.

He told me, "Go and get the book of Saint Nikiforos the Leper and he will help you." To be honest, that was the first time I had ever even heard of Saint Nikiforos. I read the book and was very deeply moved by his life. I prayed to him about our problem, we somehow came up with 5,000 euros, and my husband received his pension. Great is the grace of the saint.

Anonymous
Thessaloniki

October 27, 2013

I live in Melbourne, Australia.

In February of 2013, one of my cousins from Athens sent me a book about Saint Nikiforos the Leper.

The day I received the book I read about half of it. That evening, as I was getting ready for bed, I was seized with a terrible headache that caused excruciating pain.

I remembered the miracles of Saint Nikiforos that I had just read earlier that day and fervently begged him to help me.

Without delay, within seconds, the pain stopped and my headache was completely gone! May we have his blessing.

A.A.

Father Nicholas Sigalas from Santorini related: For years now I have held Saint Nikiforos the Leper in great esteem. Moreover, I had a personal experience of his healing intervention in the case of a nun with whom I am acquainted.

This nun had a serious skin disease on her legs and sought the help of Saint Nikiforos. She venerated his holy relics, made the sign of the Cross over her legs with the relics and miraculously became well.

March 1, 2014

My name is A.K. and I serve as a caretaker at the Church of the Annunciation of the Theotokos in Emporium, Santorini.

Towards dawn on the 3rd of January in the year 2012, I saw in my sleep an ascetic figure, venerable in

appearance, who told me, "My name is Nikiforos and tomorrow is my feast day." On the morning of January 3rd we celebrated the Divine Liturgy at our church. In the evening after Vespers I related my dream to our parish priest, asking him if there is a saint by the name of Nikiforos whose feast is celebrated around that time. He replied that there is a Martyr Saint Nikiforos who is commemorated on February 9th and also a Confessor Saint Nikiforos, Patriarch of Constantinople, who is commemorated on June 2nd. When he saw that I was insisting on a Saint Nikiforos whose feast day was in the month of January, he told me, "Indeed, there is another saint, Nikiforos the Leper, and I have a special reverence for him. He reposed on January 4th but has not yet been canonized by our Ecumenical Patriarchate and for that reason we cannot officially celebrate his memory. Furthermore, we do not have his complete Service."

Ever since this incident occurred—in other words, from the moment the saint appeared to me—I, too, honor this newly revealed Saint Nikiforos and pray to him, asking for his intercessions in whatever problems I face.

February 9, 2014

A few months ago, I somehow came across the book, *Saint Nikiforos the Leper*. This was the first time I had even heard of the saint's existence.

As I began to leaf through the pages and read about the saint's life, I stopped at the photograph of his tonsure at the Leper Community of Chios.

When I saw those big, serious and profound eyes gazing at me, I felt that this image captured the purity of his soul. From that moment, a great yearning developed within my heart to depict this image as an icon.

I imagined myself in that little church on the island, where this young man, with exceptional reverence and piety, in complete recognition of his responsibility, received the blessed monastic schema. He faithfully served the schema with his whole being, as is apparent, until the very last moment of his life, loving deeply both God and his fellow man.

I do not know if I was able to convey the majesty of this soul to any extent in this icon. But I do know that as I proceeded with the iconography, a faint yet exquisite aroma often accompanied the process. It was especially fragrant in the afternoons as I stood before the icon to examine it and see how it was turning out.

The evening the icon was completed, the same exquisite aroma flooded the room and filled my whole being. I thank the saint for visiting me.

N.N.

Athens

SACRED ICONS

of our Holy and God-bearing Father,
Nikiforos the Leper & Wonderworker